The Revolving City

51 POEMS & THE STORIES BEHIND THEM

The Revolving City

51 POEMS & THE STORIES BEHIND THEM

EDITED BY WAYDE COMPTON & RENÉE SAROJINI SAKLIKAR

anvil
PRESS

50 SFU 1965 2015 | SFU SIMON FRASER UNIVERSITY ENGAGING THE WORLD

Copyright © 2015 the Authors

Anvil Press Publishers Inc.
P.O. Box 3008, Main Post Office
Vancouver, B.C. V6B 3X5 Canada
www.anvilpress.com

Library and Archives Canada Cataloguing in Publication

    The revolving city : 51 poems and the stories behind them / Wayde Compton
& Renée Sarojini Saklikar.

Co-published by: SFU Public Square.
ISBN 978-1-77214-032-3 (paperback)

    1. Canadian poetry (English)--British Columbia--Vancouver. 2. Canadian
poetry (English)--21st century. I. Compton, Wayde, 1972-, editor II. Saklikar,
Renee Sarojini, 1962-, editor

PS8295.7.V35R49 2015   C811'.6080971133   C2015-905293-9

Cover design by Derek von Essen
Interior design by Monica Miller
Cover image: "Tioga Pass," acrylic, ink, found photograph on panel, 11 x 9 inches, 2010 by Mary Iverson

Represented in Canada by Publishers Group Canada.

Distributed in Canada by Raincoast and in the U.S. by Small Press Distribution (SPD).

The publisher gratefully acknowledges the financial assistance of the Canada Council for the Arts, the Canada Book Fund, and the Province of British Columbia through the B.C. Arts Council and the Book Publishing Tax Credit.

Printed and bound in Canada.

TO THOSE WHO MAKE TIME
AND SPACE FOR POETRY

We would like to acknowledge that Vancouver is located on unceded
Indigenous land belonging to the Coast Salish peoples.

 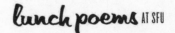

Contents

Preface

Three years ago over a casual dinner conversation with Renée Sarojini Saklikar, the idea for Lunch Poems at SFU was born. I'm not a poet, nor did I have any real affinity for poetry, but that conversation and the subsequent poetry reading with Renée opened a window into a world that neither I, nor many of my fellow colleagues at SFU Public Square, had explored.

The idea for Lunch Poems was simple. We would take over a public space at Simon Fraser University's vibrant downtown campus for a monthly poetry reading. We would pair seasoned and emerging poets in an interactive and intimate exchange and we would invite the public to join us over their lunch hour. We adopted the name Lunch Poems in honour of Frank O'Hara and his book *Lunch Poems*. The inaugural reading took place on March 28, 2012, and featured Vancouver's Poet Laureate Evelyn Lau, SFU alumna and poet Daniela Elza, and more than 100 listeners.

I'm not sure any of us expected the idea to take root, but a small group of passionate volunteers ensured that it did. Through the expert curation of SFU Writer's Studio Director, Wayde Compton, the far-reaching literary networks of Renée Sarojini Saklikar and the logistical and communication brilliance of Kim Gilker and Robin Prest, Lunch Poems grew into a community. It expanded from a monthly reading series featuring a distinctly West Coast community of poets (complete with the ambient noise of catering trollies crossing tile floors in SFU Harbour Centre), to include a website with audio recordings of our featured poets musing on their writing processes.

At the same time Lunch Poems was making its debut, the SFU Public Square was launched, with the goal to embody Simon Fraser University's vision as Canada's most community-engaged research university. For our first Community Summit in 2012, we partnered with Vancouver Foundation to focus on the theme of isolation and disconnection in the urban environment. The end result, *Alone Together: Connecting in the City*, reached far and wide to explore issues as diverse as the future of libraries in communities and the role of Metro Vancouver mayors in creating community connections. Lunch Poems reflected similar beliefs in the importance of engagement across community and cultural divides, so when the idea was raised for a Lunch Poems poetry anthology, the theme of urban experience seemed like a natural fit.

The Revolving City: 51 Poems and the Stories Behind Them also includes author reflections that allow the reader to dig deeper into the story behind the poem. In addition to sharing their poetry, the Lunch Poems poets have shared their inspiration and motivation, making this anthology unique and accessible—especially for readers like myself who are unaccustomed to poetry.

From its humble origins, Lunch Poems at SFU has taken shape and established itself as a premier showcase for West Coast and Canadian poetry. This anthology, featuring work from many past Lunch Poems poets, captures the pulse and intention behind our original series. Editors Wayde Compton and Renée Sarojini Saklikar, with the support and stewardship of managing editor Monica Miller, have tapped the spirit and intensity of "the poetry reading that could" and amplified these poetic voices beyond our SFU walls.

In 2015, SFU celebrates its 50th birthday. What better way to mark this important milestone than to shine new light on the works of this brilliant community of poets.

SHAUNA SYLVESTER
Director, SFU Centre for Dialogue
Executive Director, SFU Public Square

Introductions

At the Lunch Poems reading series we have featured up to twenty poets a year since 2012. (Though at the time of publication our Lunch Poems series continues, this anthology could only include poets who read for us in 2012-14.) Some of the poets are local and some from afar, some with their first manuscript or debut book in hand and others who have written dozens of books, some lyrical, some experimental, and none of them fitting easily into any simple category. Each poem presented here is followed by the poet's discussion of its creation. Our goal has always been to be aesthetically ecumenical: to feature poets who are pursuing form from a variety of positions, concerns, and cultural perspectives.

The original intention of the Lunch Poems series was to offer a midday and mid-week meditation on poetry in the heart of downtown. So the series has always been thoughtfully disruptive, like poetry itself, erupting out of the quotidian and delivering something deliberate and defamiliar in the centre of the proscribed space of work. Like the natural interruption of lunch, poetry too, we say, is a necessity. Make time for it. Carve out space for it. Put it at the centre and let the world accommodate its presence.

WAYDE COMPTON

To live in the city, is to experience dichotomy: east/west, alone/together: architecture as exploration of class, ecology as a means of production. More and more, we might see the city as ecosphere, habitat where the disparate might meet, even if by no other means than happenstance or necessity, where inside, the interiority of self, collides with, confronts, and sometimes embraces, outside, the external reality or, perhaps, illusion. The only way to encounter, is through self-body-culture.

Here we find the poet: a wayfinder into the city and outside its boundaries, pockets filled with words, or empty, and underneath, around, behind each poem, we readers might discern an urgency: how to reconcile individual to collective, how to embrace/reject. All this happening/not happening in a conversation thousands of years old and fresh as the latest tweet: what does it mean to be alive, right now? What separates us? What draws us together?

Long ago, I once read that the early Greeks posited the world as amalgam: nature, society, history, self. And that the self, body, mind, soul interwove with the world, indivisible. Was it Cicero who perceived the city as a new artefact, separate from? I neither confirm nor deny.

The poets in this collection take us both inward, into the private joys and hurts of the individual and the family, and outward into a world of conflict and connection, a nexus of locations: past, present, the future. In concept and form, these poems investigate belonging/not belonging, and in so doing, pinpoint markers for our greatest challenge: how to live without destroying ourselves or this planet, all this taken on within the realm of that endless field, a page of words.

Reader, may you find here much soul nourishment, delight, may you find provocation and questions, and may you be unsettled by the echo of our living in this turbulent time, the end of an age, the beginning of—

RENÉE SAROJINI SAKLIKAR

DAPHNE MARLATT

through cloud

through cloud

                                   white shock blue Grouse willow ware
shades glaze those two facing Sisters hyas muckamuck
renamed couchant imperial untracked Crown looms legalized
so close down Main tonight hope snows veins eyes loose
change names liquid

                                drip eaves long gone in re-
build demolished reconstructed viz city market dream the
locals by early water under bridge no willow sole perch
sturgeon at False Creek points slaughterhouse then sawmill
muck
        mark it
                  a market econ oh

who managing whose house it runs down to

                                     e-merge

a metro built on labour's back on brick or wood slats glitz
'n bling now wallow in stock collapse concrete drips snow
line no-show line down blue shopping or shipping out all
water under the bridge

                        capitalized on

Suezmax tanker traffic liquid asset runoff
liquid(i)city
                's melt oolichan near gone

it's warming up
                so grab a

rainhat eh once cedar see reigning oil's long
reach it rains for free

               still

                    it rains

What lies behind "through cloud"?

When I was writing *Vancouver Poems* (Coach House, 1972), I was a young woman writing my way into the city I had adopted as home but wanted to meet in some depth. The contemporary feel of streets, bridges, beaches, parks; the storied residue of people from earlier decades reaching back to pre-settlement time. Taking the measure of the city in phrases ranging from colloquial to reportorial. Measure as the rhythm of phrases in quick succession breaking into an isolated word or phrase, a line that looks like prose but isn't.

This rhythm syncopates in "through cloud," written more recently for *Liquidities: Vancouver Poems Then and Now* (Talonbooks, 2013). This poem breaks the line to highlight a contrast between the continuing presence of mountains, sea, rain, and the rapid (rapacious) changes of urban development at the expense of biosphere. There's an ironic and double-edged reference to "house," Greek *oicos* (house) at the root of ecology, and how obliviously at home we make ourselves in our impermanent constructions.

Language plays run through this poem that began very simply with a desire to register the "white shock" of snow-capped mountains appearing after days of being hidden in cloud. That visual image, white on blue, inverts the Chinoiserie pattern known as willow ware, which raises the issue of cultural import, imposition. Remembering the Squamish name, translated as The Sisters (Pauline Johnson), for The Lions, the descriptive current is stopped by recognition of imperialism (oh those British lions) and our earlier governments' attempt to erase First Nations culture and land rights. So there's a cultural mix here (in poem as in city), from hyas muckamuck (a Chinook term used in 19th century trade) to Crown, another British imperial name. The poem's perspective then shifts closer to home, to Main Street where "snow" is a commodity in Downtown Eastside street trade. So the poem continues, shift upon shift, until it runs down to rain.

EVELYN LAU

Solitary

Last night a visitor came to the prison cell
of my apartment, sipped her drink
as if in a dream, her underwater eyes signalling
claustrophobia, and when I said I'd lived here
ten years her mouth opened in shock—
but it was night, she couldn't see
the shrubs standing sentry on the rooftop garden,
the branches with their kernel buds
firing one by one into leaf,
how day after day I tell myself there is still
time. Here in the centre of the city
where the trees are storm clouds
planted along the pavement,
and the sky is splintered with high-rises,
seagulls circle the back alleys
and the barnacled marina, screaming
for scraps, and in the distance there is a view
reflected from a sun-fired window.

These silent afternoons
of books and poetry, when heat sits in the locked room
as in a lion's mouth where I write,
I begin to make of my life
a meditation, the life I tried to rid
myself of for so long—
even as a fly on the windowsill
scrubs its face with brisk motions
and down the hall a door closes,
opens, closes for good.

—◊—

"Solitary" was written in my early thirties, a time when one feels on the cusp of a decision—get married and lead a more secure, conventional life, or turn into the Cat Lady? Well, it's now a decade later and I've lived in the same tiny condo for 20 years. Poetry demands solitude, and time for contemplation. In a phenomenally expensive city like Vancouver, it has meant giving up dreams of owning a house, among other material comforts, to hunker down in my little apartment, clipping coupons and eating expired food. At the same time, it's a luxurious life—living downtown, every possible convenience is steps away, and so is the seawall and the ocean. Some writers live in sprawling homes on acreage hours away from the nearest town; that sort of solitude would drive me bonkers in a day. Solitude in the middle of a bustling city seems to suit my process; I crave the rich inner life that comes from living alone, but thrive on the contrast of having the world just outside my front door.

Woman Dining Alone

Don't mistake her:
She is not lonely scattered over there
with her books and napkins,
not escaping marital dread.

She loves her husband, daughter.
Neither is she on the make
posing with the soup d'jour
diffident over bread and butter
glancing up to see who is looking
at a woman dining alone.

Eating can be (they say) satisfaction
of animal need, communal act.
Yet this (don't turn your heads
at the arrival of the entrée)
this is her hour of repose
between candle and journal,
a savouring of the inner life
that goes on so much of the time
without her.

And if with a fork in one hand
and a pen in the other
she scribbles words in that small black book,
she is not an artiste.
Words too are her nourishment.

—◊—

Inner and outer, public and private, self and other, contemplation and action. I am both an introvert and a communal being. How to find the balance between these apparent polarities in the midst of urban life has emerged as a theme in my work over the years.

"Woman Dining Alone" is a poem written when I was in my late forties with an eight-year-old child and a full-time teaching job. I was a late-life mom who had experienced many years of solitude before finding a life mate, and so I sometimes found the traditional role of mother challenging. I felt I had to fight for a space for my writing.

This poem is feminist in the sense of refusing my mother's and some relatives' notion that if a woman dined alone she looked vulnerable at best, at worst, like a woman "on the make," hungry for a man. After all, if eating is a communal activity, then a woman dining alone advertises that she might be partner-less, pitiable. Of course, things have changed greatly for women since I wrote the poem but not enough, and not for all women.

On this occasion, my husband and daughter were away on a camping trip. I could hunker in my own *temenos* or sacred space right in the middle of the everyday clatter. I deliberately chose an elegant restaurant with white tablecloths and candles in a heritage house, and found myself a quiet nook near the fireplace.

To this day, I love the paradox of being alone in a public-private space. The background din, the clatter and chatter becomes a nest for my writing rather than a distraction. Cafés with books are still my idea of paradise. Gurus and mindfulness masters may chide us for multi-tasking, but for me, eating, reading, and ruminating in solitude are part of a single motion.

KIM MINKUS

In a house of glass I listen to my bird. it is night
rather than morning. the library glows—only screens
no paper nor people. days are no longer divided into meals.
written words have given way to green
and night has no documents. the rooms are empty
weeks lay ahead of us with nothing but planting

my bird sings—*we gather everything*
from our gardens. he pecks at words
and sneaks loamy garden terms into his breath
no decay. merely night gardening and
the crackle of bugs burrowing into soil

the bird and I trace the names of those with money
the rich play on porches, in mountains
our flight takes us into paths that were once roads
now filled with flowers and jewelled planters

When I sat down to write "Bird," I had just finished reading the essay "Iconography" by Matthew Soules in the collection *Vancouver Matters*. This collection features essays from architects, artists, and academics that examine the "successes and failures" of Vancouver as a city. What was of particular interest to me in Soules' research was his definition of the terms "eco-metropolis" and "boutique urbanism." Soules identified Vancouver as a small (boutique) city whose success at integrating nature and urbanity made it highly marketable on the global stage.

I had been developing a poem that imagined a future Vancouver where an "exclusive" green lifestyle dominated, and I wanted to traverse this imagined city just as poet Lisa Robertson did in her "SEVEN WALKS," but I wanted to "fly" over it. Robertson's reference to "my guide" in her poetic essay gives a nod to Virgil's appearance as guide in Dante's *Divine Comedy*. I began to wonder who would guide me in my flight. Chaucer's *House of Fame* had always resonated with me and the first line of my poem, "In a house of glass," alludes to this work; the "glass" referring both to the glass temple in Chaucer's poem and Vancouver's modern towers. Chaucer's poem has been described as a parody of the *Divine Comedy*; a dream vision that features the poet being guided by an eagle. All of these influences coalesced and my guide also became a bird, one I imagined as a raven, clutching me in its claws and flying me over my future city. The poem criticizes present-day Vancouver, where homes are unaffordable for all but the wealthy, and also imagines a future Vancouver where libraries are vast living computers having lost their community role for the poor and marginalized. In this future Vancouver the "green elite" play "on porches, in mountains."

TIM BOWLING

Walking Through a North American City, the Tenderman Picks Up a Rhythm

Conform (Do your own thing) Conform (Do your own thing)
Something sinister in the schoolyard
The sky's the colour of spider-catch
Do your own thing (Conform) Do your own thing (Conform)
Down at the parlours, tattooing fresh meat
Down at the parlours, tattooing fresh meat
I Love Mom on a joint and a hock
I Love Mom in the rib of an eye
Conform (Do your own thing) Conform
Nobody's got any time for Time
The astronomer hasn't got any space
I got a sad letter from a childhood friend
so I emailed him a couple of lines
I got a sad letter from a childhood friend
so I emailed him a couple of lines
Will you be buried or will you be burned?
Conform your own thing conform
Will you be ashes or food for the worms?
Be your own cancer conform
Do your own stroke conform
Will you be ashes or food for the worms?

Man is in chains before he is born.

—◊—

This poem attempts to face head-on the rhetoric about individualism, free will, and work so prevalent in North American life. Along with Adrienne Rich, I tend to believe that "no one tells the truth about truth." But why don't we? Because it's too disappointing to accept that we're just like everyone else? Because the most important body modification decision is the ultimate one about ashes and worms? Because our children (born into a poisoned biosphere and various forms of institutionalized prejudice) are chained before we conceive them? I guess I must have answered yes to all these questions when I wrote the poem, but the poet in me, as the poet always seeks to do, looked for a way to sing the answer. The result is a kind of musical raised-middle-finger to a society that diverts itself with trivial amusements while the same old bastards who control the money and the power prattle on about the same old freedom and patriotism. So, hello ghost of Rousseau, would you like a tattoo of that tenet on your ectoplasm?

RAHAT KURD

April Is When I Most Hate Vancouver

To the sudden brightening
of gilded limbs fatly festooned,

some ancestral being must have blinked awake
and, to the edge of sickness, swooned

with the desire to be young again.
To spin the sugar, and colour it like that

some hungry merchant must have dreamed
of selling clouds suffused with evening light

in sticky miniature, a twenty-five cent fantasia
melting to sweet grit in the teeth.

But here some bitterer ephemera
fills my mouth. Think of the vital sap

sucked up the riven green-furred trunk,
urging the buds, *effloresce*

as the tough root's stealth campaign for longevity
in a colour Germaine Greer wants outlawed

for soothing girls and women with the lie, *fate's roseate*—
warm as lips tracing a persuasive

line of flattery down your neck, past the crook of your arm;
swearing to your fingertips that for beauty

you'll never go hungry again; that's rent money
in bloom; pay no attention to the storm

that strips the branches, swirls and flutters
the blushing tender, forces the wedding

in scurrilous haste, to hailstones. Glory
hardly realized; glory already squandered,

pulped into ruin, into every cracked grey line
of the city you keep waking up from,

the party you're always late to,
arriving always fearful

the musicians have left the floor
to the sweeper's broom's silence;

the wantable stranger, already turned away:
shoulders hunched, massive, snow-dusted,

eyes only for the ocean,
while you stare, stupid, famished,

believing in cherries, until not one faint scent
umbrellas the cloudburst upon your head.

I had failed at everything. All I wanted now was a place where I could sit down to collect my thoughts, and I was failing at that too. Every coffee shop I stopped to look into was full of people with their notebooks or laptops open. They sipped coffee, serene, virtuous, industriously at work. They were where they wanted to be. They had made the right sorts of decisions in life. My failure to find a seat among them; the fact that I was still searching; that I had not already been at work for several hours by mid-morning, that the wind was now kicking up and rain would shortly begin spattering; all seemed connected to the decisions I had made eons ago as an optimistic young woman, decisions only now ripening into truth; in fact, everywhere I looked I saw them bursting into menacing, tightly packed, fat, flaunting masses of spectacular wrongness. *I was wrong to get married*, they jeered from every branch; *I was wrong to move to Vancouver*, they threatened, in a colour that nearly gouged my eyes out on every street. I wrenched open the door of one last coffee place. No one else was there. I didn't notice how sullen the young woman who took my order appeared at first. But after I sat down and pulled out my notebook, the stereo speakers above my head erupted in screeches, throbs, and wails, conveying deep hatred of all humanity and the pointlessness of being alive. Rain fell. I stared out the window at a tall, spindly cherry tree, mobbed with pink blossoms that shook and shook.

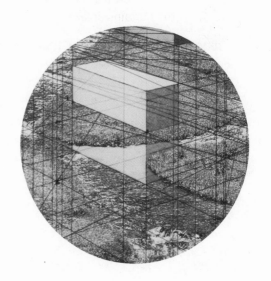

getting the *story/line* in order

perhaps it was only a dream
          when your home left you in a hurry

before the morning light
          left the door open
      the curtains ablaze
with sunrise.

the space between us cluttered with
          little feuds.
they have grown now.   you should see them.

they chase dust bunnies around
       are asking for water and solid food.

and the doctor?
       she could not find anything wrong
with you.   after x-rays   and ultrasounds

       she sent you   *home.*

at the traffic light an arm hangs out of a car window
flicks a cigarette butt into the shadows of
          your panic
      sets something ablaze
in the dark entrance of your loss.

while the tree   across the street of   your desire
is covered in decades of   city dust and grime

is backed up against a warehouse wall
       anticipating its firing squad.

a lamppost on the street stands   sentinel—
a soldier with his helmet on.

stands before the window of your abandonment.

you listen to his stories.   said: he gave up
his weapons for a good cause.

you could not understand the words *giving up* or
what *good* meant. or if there is something we
should have declared to each other—

    or how your voice turned transgression
how you were held   hostage
                in the ambiguity of his gaze.

those little acts of warfare that first begin
                         within ourselves.

➤

the doctor could not find anything   wrong
with you.   sent you *home*.

        and you   went looking for it.

that night you slept
    on the stacked tables of your worries
behind the folded chairs of your *together*
               piled high   as grief.

               this party is over.

all night the wind runs its fingers through
the hair of your sorrow.
        whispers fables in your ears.

your eyes—grown accustomed to a darkness
that descended for years.

did not know how much more you are yet
to lose. did not know someone was watching

tallying your wrong moves   your missteps
the words you never meant. stacking them high

like folded chairs and tables.

—∿—

This poem is an excerpt from a longer sequence written to the photography exhibit *Story/Line* by Larry Wolfson, displayed by the Sidney and Gertrude Zack Gallery in Vancouver (December, 2013). The four fragments here incorporate a number of the images from the exhibit. When I walked into the gallery I was doggedly followed by the grief of a separation. I was coming to the realization that my efforts to keep my family together were to no avail. I was trying to make sense of what was happening to me. The images apprehended me, leapt at me, and in that moment became vehicles for loss. They helped crystallize the conflicting feelings about where, and what, is *home*. For years I heard what my mind had to say, those were default thoughts of the day. Now, I wanted to learn what the heart thought. It was circling in these sensations like a puppy looking for a place to lie down. It was happy to locate itself in these images. They became containers. I kept filling them. The initial piece was written on the spot, followed by a week of intense editing. One row of words, one row of tears. Reading it in public a week later in the gallery for *the art and poetry* event was terrifying. Writing, for me, has always helped me make better and more compassionate sense. More importantly, it helps me reimagine new possibilities.

The Dreams We Take For Silence

Trees that leaned tall and sweet yesterday afternoon
are gone. All that new sky bleeding blue mocks me.
Last week there were lilacs standing twelve feet tall
swirling their blossoms free in the wind, scratching their names on the day
the cloud of their scent blotting out the neighbours.

I remember when this was the field where Jevon and Peter played,
built their secret rocket ships, dreamt of who-knows-what
now it's overgrown with rows of perfect identical homes
probably filled with perfect identical families.

The boundaries of these well-groomed plots border on pretension
no room left for envy when everything looks the same.
The shortcuts and byways have all been replaced
by squared-off yards smoothed flat with lawns, trimmed
in conventional styles: just so many haircuts in a row.

Everyone lies aligned, awake in their king-size beds
warmed by the light of flickering blue hypnosis
trying to think of one more gadget to buy.

Because I've lived in the same neighbourhood for more than 20 years, I've witnessed a slew of changes to the place. Among the most difficult of these has been the loss of trees and green space. But perhaps even more problematic has been the demise of what we used to call "vacant lots." As a walker, the disappearance of these unoccupied spaces means the shortcuts I once relied upon no longer exist.

I'll admit that I may have used some poetic license in building the details of this poem. For one thing, it isn't always lilacs that are cut down. However, they're flowers that everyone knows, with a fragrance most people recognize. And where scent is one of our most powerful memory-triggers, lilac seemed appropriate as the shrubbery being cut down in the first section—all those sweet memories torn away with just a few swipes of a chainsaw.

The scene of the vacant lot with small boys playing (one of them my son) is meant to further nudge the reader's memory, possibly evoking a sense of nostalgia. I never knew exactly what Jevon and Peter did in their "fort" but I remembered some of the crazy inventions my friends and I had fooled around with as kids (rocket ships powered by sulphur match-heads we'd chopped from hundreds of wooden matches). Thus, I presumed rockets as one of their experiments. Besides, aren't rockets the stuff of dreams? I'll bet Chris Hadfield would agree.

Yet the contrast by poem's end reveals a place where dreams are no longer of "secret rocket ships" but instead have become consumer-fuelled fantasies. The neighbourhood has transformed from being a place where kids can engage in imaginative play and morphed into a tract of identical houses where people spend their time indoors. Even the blue of the sky has been replaced with the "flickering blue" light of late-night infomercials.

BETSY WARLAND

Excerpt from *Oscar of Between, Part 17A*

He boards the BART train midday at Oakland City Center. Stands tentatively just inside the sliding doors. Small man lost in layers and layers of clothing and too-large parka. To his immediate left, a young mother holds picture-perfect daughter on her lap. A few feet in front of him, Oscar and Ingrid sit. As soon as the doors close he begins in a quiet voice. "I'm so afraid. I don't know what to do. I'm afraid of me. And afraid what I might do to you…" The mother (rigid with fear) deftly moves her hands slowly up to cover daughter's ears. Oscar peripherally sees others' eyes are fixed on floor, windows, mobile devices. Only other African American in the car—a well-dressed, handsome, professional man in his thirties with attaché case—stares straight ahead. Oscar takes the risk of letting him see she's listening. "I'm afraid of me. Afraid of you. I don't know what to do. I'm so afraid. I can't go on like this. I'm so afraid … afraid what I might do to you." The train approaches the next station, slows (will he get off? take this further?). Halts. People gingerly walk around him to exit. Just before doors close he slips out. A perceptible sigh moves through the car. The mother's hands drop to hug her daughter. Conversations tentatively begin here & there. Oscar and Ingrid quietly comment on how profound his despair was—how he speaks for so very many—then fall back into silence.

I write with a poet's sensibilities and strategies but for almost two decades have been writing lyric prose. What still shapes me is how the very form of the poem signals urgency! Something bursts out as contrasted to the sprawl of prose. The poem's urgency is manifest by the use of extreme compression: much is left out. The poem depends on us to read between the lines and blank spaces; decipher its body language; feel our complicity. "The poem enters your head like an idea enters your mind." (*Breathing the Page: Reading the Act of Writing*). If the poem is to be of value—it must repeatedly stand at the threshold of awe— wonder, dread, astonishment, fear. So why have I not clearly remained a poet? I'm obsessed with how states of consciousness fold and unfold personally as well as publically: prose accommodates this circuitous, ongoing narrative quest and investigation.

In 2007, I began writing *Oscar of Between* (http://www.betsywarland.com/ excerpts-from-oscar-of-between/). With this manuscript I assumed a new narrative position: a person of between. Not only did it suit the nature of this narrative, it was also the first time a narrative position totally suited me. In *Oscar of Between*, I write in various forms of the public voice (as understood in the U.K.) while I investigate what has shaped my personal voice. We are living in a complex global environment tittering on numerous scenarios of chaos, creativity and collapse. Moral courage is crucial if we are to move beyond reactivity, disappearing into our electronic devices, expunging difference. U.S. author Sarah Schulman recently said, "Pretending that a human being does not exist, that their experience doesn't matter, is the centrepiece of the world's pain."[1]

---

[1] *Herizons*, Fall 2014, Vol. 28, No. 2 page 43.

Tomorrow

Forever we push carts along dirt roads of counts in tomorrow, make birds into stones and move the rocks so that when they vibrate they spring to life, make chickens, roasts, tomatoes that are too modified to produce organs.

Friday we walk the streets of rain and grey coats the bottoms of pant legs. We can't wash the grey out, we'll have to bleach our eyes and teeth again. Put the coin on my lips, I'll use it for the laundry later.

When you call I hear someone else speaking. The Scarecrow asking for his brains, the zombie requesting Facebook friendship, but my flesh has been devoured so I can only poke back with bones.

Forget the video game men, square chests cut.

When the government came asking for money, I apologized and said I had no change left. I only use debit.

I followed you, falsely.

When we wear our costumes, you have birds flocking you, landing on the tips of your fingers. When I stick my fingers out, they pick the nails or ignore friend requests.

You have one mutual friend with yourself.

Saturday we boil our guts with beer and call for cabs that will take us to cabs. You'll recount the wine that has stained your skin and I'll recount the ways. When we arrive at the ocean, we find it empty again. Someone flushed the earth and seaweed lays dried like flowers for death.

I had a career in careerism until I lost it all when the precession hit.

When you call, I can hear my mother's voice, she asks for flour. I can't quite eat the pie or else my irritable bowel will talk about the time he quaked the silos.

Or this is just another poem about you.

Saturday, we couldn't get past, it just went on and on. When all the Fridays and Thursdays died off, we couldn't find any more bars to drink. We just sat at the beginning of Saturday hoping the sun would set to make way for Sunday, but Sunday called in terminally sick or had to take permanent stress leave. Annie is still singing about tomorrow.

If I close my eyes I see the world in which would have been—had you the ability to regenerate body. I fail and fail and fail, at least this world has your hands.

—⁓—

This poem was a free-write that was based around Vancouver being a port city. The stem of the poem, for me, is about globalization and what that means for our interpersonal relationships. At the time, I was dealing with a very sick mother and the failing end of a relationship, and trying to process this in a city that is renowned for its natural beauty. Reflecting on how the city works, and how globalization works, I was interested in looking at the idea of costumes and performance. Some of us are very good at performing in a capitalist-driven world, and some of us flounder. When I was writing the poem I wanted the poem to begin in the middle with the line, "You have one mutual friend with yourself," and expanding from there, making two poems. But if I'm going to be really honest, this poem is actually about you.

Immigration

To escape from the tyrannical logic
　　Of your mother tongue
You wandered, wandering
　　　Through earth's length and breadth
　　Subjecting your old self to another syntax
A whole set of grammatical rules
　　　Strangely new to your lips and tips
　　To expand the map of your mind
　　　Far beyond your home and haven
Yet in the meantime it becomes colonized
　　　By all the puzzling paradoxes
　　Of this chosen language, for example:
　　　Quicksand can be very slow
　　　Boxing rings are in fact square
　　　And a guinea pig is neither a pig
　　　Nor is it from Guinea
　　　　　Like you or me

"Immigration" is not only one of the first but also the very best poems I have ever composed since I began to write poetry in English during a family tour to Banff in 2004. Thematically inspired by Laiwan's poem "The Imperialism of Syntax" and linguistically informed by Peter Legge's speech "English is a Crazy Language," this piece exemplifies the kind of poetry I most love to write and read: short, experimental and suggestive. Into the grammatical fabric of this work I tried to weave my feelings and observations about the transient, transnational and even transcendental experiences every immigrant might undergo at a given spot of time. Through this poem, I hope to reveal that all of us are immigrants in the broad sense of the word. Indeed, as we constantly move to live in a new languacultural environment, both our physical and spiritual life may be exposed to something profoundly ironic and enlightening. Undoubtedly, such exposure has practical as well as philosophical significance. Among more than 100 "parallel poems" I have written to emulate the original, "Immigration" is certainly satisfying to me as a poetry scribbler and perhaps even to some literary critics; otherwise, it would never have been selected as reading material for a 100-level English course at the University of Alberta in 2005–06 shortly after its initial appearance in *Other Voices*.

Stuff to do When Your Hometown is Burning

1. Finish up your cup of tea before it gets cold because you know you hate it cold.

2. Think about calling your mother.

3. Don't call your mother. She'll freak out. Asking questions like hail pelting down, like pepper sneezed into your face, like unrelenting projectile vomit on your recently cleaned carpet. Don't call you mother. She'll freak out as if you knew much more than the headlines proclaim: Gulu is in Flames.

4. Change the channel. Change. Change. Change. Nothing. None of the news media will carry it, and why should they? Gulu is burning, but does not even warrant a lined script flowing at the bottom of your TV screen.

5. Return to the internet site. Read the article again. Gulu is Burning. Still burning. Same title renders the burning a continuous and never-ending act— Gulu is hell.

6. Email a friend. Enclose the link.

7. Read your friend's response—oh dear.

8. Oh dear you, oh dear me, oh dear everything around you—scattered books on the table, papers, receipts from a cup of coffee and muffin that you hated, the latest *O Magazine* proclaiming secrets to a long and joyful life complete with beautiful skin—your hometown is burning.

9. The dishes are stacked up in the sink. They always are. Grape stalks on the kitchen counter, coffee grinds on the floor by the trash can. A damp kitchen cloth. Your hometown is burning.

10. The face of a woman you know appears on the computer devoid of any apparent emotion. What does it feel like when your hometown is burning? How can you show it? Where are the T-shirts, the arm bands, the YouTube clips, the tweets, the letter writers, the dissenters, the peace lovers, the protesters, the batons, the loudspeakers, the police, the guns, the tear gas, the burning tires in the middle of the road, the pickup trucks, goons throwing politicians to the back of the track and speeding away? Where are the signs that your hometown is burning?

11. Pink and yellow tulips in a vase. Not any less gorgeous, even as dead stalks that cling to any semblance of life—opening up to the light through the blinds and closing up in the evening, sucking at what juices might be mixed in the water.

12. Wash some dishes.

13. Shower.

14. Fix your hair.

15. Wear lipstick.

16. Remember to take your shades—it's sunny outside.

17. Call your mother.

18. Listen to your mother freak out just like you thought she would. Why should this be happening to us again, why? When did it start? Who is doing this? Not again, she wails, not again.

19. Gulu is in flames as the fourth division pours out into the streets showing firepower, manly power, deadly, manly firepower.

20. Your hometown is burning. So you take the bus, go to work, mark papers, submit a short story and think about dinner.

On April 16, 2011, both major Ugandan national newspapers, *New Vision* and *Daily Monitor* carried headlines on the deadly walk-to-work protests in my hometown of Gulu. These protests had begun earlier in the year, led by a political opposition leader, Kizza Besigye, to protest the high costs of fuel and food. The Ugandan government had reacted firmly, with the army called in to tear gas, beat protesters and even use rubber bullets. Several people in the capital city Kampala were hurt, including a pregnant woman who was hauled into the back of a truck and taken away, and the fatal shooting of a two-year-old. It was only in Gulu that the Fourth Division of the Uganda People's Defence Force used live bullets and killed three people at the protests. The leader of the Democratic Party, Nobert Mao, was roughed up and arrested.

In April, 2011, loads of things were happening internationally. Hosni Mubarak, the former Egyptian president had resigned earlier that month, motioning towards the dominoes of protests that would eventually spread across Africa and the Middle East. Watching these events from the west coast, the same as I've been watching the events that take place in Uganda for most of my adult life was and is an uncanny experience. You feel as if you know and yet you don't know, can't know what it is to be there. It is unsettling; it disrupts the otherwise regular flow of your day, making it impossible to disregard the relationship between the flutter in your belly and the storm at home. There is an undeniable connection beyond nostalgia, whether one admits it to others or not.

When I read about the walk-to-work protests, I imagined that peaceful resistance to the Ugandan government was a sign that the system was working out its kinks. Details like rubber bullets and tear gas matched the security organs from other protest cities, as did the seemingly brand new army uniforms, bulletproof vests, batons, face shields, shiny black boots and remarkable restraint, considering. Sometimes a moment like Cairo can be imagined everywhere—people have the power, the people are the power. So what happens when the people's power cannot withstand bullets, or fire, or tankers bearing down on scores of human bodies?

When I read about the the Fourth Division of the UPDF opening fire on protesters in Gulu, I got caught up in a strange vortex that remains determined by distance, modern technical advancements, and the north/south power relations between media houses that control what is and what isn't news. There it was, a national army firing on protesters with live bullets and it seemed important but it wasn't—no local or international news channel available to me was carrying it. It seemed incredulous, but it wasn't—the world around me was detached, no one was talking about it, nothing stopped to witness or commiserate. At the same time, this became a point of connection with people who remain invisible because they're defined by origins outside the navel centre, that sign of an umbilicus that used to be a lifeline but is now a focus for fascination and distraction from what else matters.

Entropic Ends

1.

"Let everything be produced, be read, become real, visible, and marked with the sign of effectiveness ..."
— Jean Baudrillard

keep no secrets
in your/our worn denim
type prior to
reply archive
achieve your/our full sense
in well-wrought
articulation maybe cry
a few tears
show you/we are serious
bleat and bleat and
press send or post
without a glance back
your/our beautiful infinite
page, see there
those blackish marks
that flash of light
is what you/we mean
to say a part of your/our
precarious heart
bleeds slightly below
maybe to the left
a glimmer of red
flickers as your/our self
as public clicks past

2.

"It is no longer a matter of making things visible to the external eye. It is rather a question of making things transparent to themselves."
— Jean Baudrillard

enrage readers
perhaps they want to harm you/us
or hurl digital insults
or one negative comment
is worth 97.5 positive ones
because who believes
the sycophants who always
like your/our hair in the photo
develop a selective way
of seeing what's being said
think of your/our readers
as losers anyway
except for your/our friends
to whom you/we can speak
with inside jokes and innuendos
chuckle visibly through punctuation
and acronyms, but close your/our
curtains to Google Earth

3.

"So, there will soon only be ... figures who ... wander alone and pass their time by perpetually telling themselves their story."
— Jean Baudrillard

or the illusion of the social
literalizes screen culture
back to the messy body
walking along an ocean
with a dog, a relentless dog
who lifts a break in the osmosis
your/our inspiring lungs suck
salty breaths transform
the air without thinking
suddenly you/we name
the liminal space and therefore
can see it colours merging
into pods that swing in trees
or shipping containers off
of ocean liners constructed
into where you/we live now

Practices of reading are even more important to me than writing. I agree with Susan Sontag when she says, "the impulse to write is almost always fired by reading." These poems were sparked by my desire to ignite my reading of Jean Baudrillard and connect it with my own ideas about the way that social media is changing how we use language. I wanted the response to be poetic because poetry is always the form that gives me the most latitude to document my thinking, the conversations that swirl in my head — me and Baudrillard out walking on the seawall, talking, arguing while the wind blows off the ocean, the glare of the glass from West End apartment buildings glinting in our eyes. The "as if" of that urban scenario.

I used the word "entropic" in the title because I think the end of things actually happens quite slowly. One small particle drifts away and gradually everything changes. The way language changes is like that too — one word drops out of favour (think: groovy) and then you can't express that particular sensibility embedded in its time quite the same way anymore. Meaning gets lost all the time. Me and Baudrillard might choose to wander, leave the seawall and get lost in the veering paths that stop making sense to map-makers. We might evade Google Earth for a minute, might discover a secret urban garden hidden in an alleyway. At some point, we'll have to account for it though. Someone will ask us where we've been and we'll have to construct a story. Our story. If we like it, we might end up telling it perpetually. Or poetically.

Elvis and Jacques

At the laundromat on Rue Saint-Viateur the proprietor looks like Elvis or at least someone who would have looked like Elvis if Elvis hadn't OD'ed on deep-fried peanut butter and banana sandwiches. He turns to me and asks, "Chaud ou froid?" I tell him, "One hot, two cold, and soap," and he passes me a small yogurt container filled with detergent and two sheets of fabric softener. I put the fabric softener into my bag and later mistake it for Kleenex on the bus to Ottawa, and don't realize this until I blow my nose and everything starts to smell like fresh pine. An Elvis collage and a display of newspaper clippings about Jacques Villeneuve cover the walls in one corner of the laundromat. The other walls are crammed with community bulletin boards containing ads for bilingual psychics, travel posters advertising an unnamed tropical destination, and notices in three languages warning customers not to overload the machines. My clothes spin around the washers, and I wonder about the punishments for overloading: my mother would make the culprits eat laundry soap, and my father would send them into the backyard to pile wood. By the time my wash cycle finishes, I feel as if my life has somehow been saved.

—⁓—

It's not every day that the proprietor of a laundromat looks like Elvis. As soon as I saw him I knew that I would end up writing about him in a poem. That was the easy part. What I didn't know right away was just how well the smaller details would help to capture that particular Montreal neighbourhood.

Many places view Elvis as an icon, but how many with a Québécois accent? And how many at the same time also celebrate race car champion Jacques Villeneuve, whose father, Gilles, was also a celebrated race car champion before his death in a racing accident? How many other cities have an Elvis surrounded by bilingual psychics, multilingual environments and tropical destination posters meant to give viewers momentary escape from hectic lives and harsh winters? The scene was new to me and I marvelled at just how harmonious it all felt.

In retrospect, my fear of overloading had more to do with a fear of interrupting that harmony, and my understanding of punishment was limited to my own personal experience. It's difficult to intuit decorum and appropriateness when you're an outsider. I knew only that all types of folks do laundry. Even Elvises. Most of us like to be clean. When that load spun its final cycle, I felt I'd passed a test.

FIONA TINWEI LAM

Shower

Those mornings you're here, the three of us
stand in a spray of soft diamonds—sunlight
through glass, and everything sparkling.
You hold our son high in your arms
while I lather him up. Our little otter,
he's as sleek and slick as when he slid
from my womb. Then I lather you,
foot to thigh, chest to back—the heft
and sinew of what I have loved. You and he both
turn in the warm rain, my universe
of prince and king rinsed to a glisten.
When you soap my skin, I live,
become brief silk in your hands, as luscious
as when your desire flowed. Only water
will love me when you are gone.

—꩜—

I've found that specific sites where certain events have occurred can inspire poems—e.g. a certain park or beach, a particular room, and in this case, the shower. Although these locations may be quite ordinary, the memories associated with them may be very strong. Something indelible, meaningful and symbolic has transpired there that calls out to be captured and expressed.

"Shower" is one of several site-inspired poems in my second poetry book that offered a way of depicting various points in a changing relationship. I tried to shape this lyric poem to be as visual, tactile, aural (e.g. assonance, alliteration, half-rhyme, rhyme, rhythm) and sensual as possible to capture the intensity of the intimacy and grief, and the intertwining of the emotional and physical that were distilled in my memories of that time and afterward.

Although "Shower" is fundamentally a poem about loss, it also frames, celebrates and commemorates a series of moments, that were real and true, where the emotional and the physical were inseparably intertwined: in a way, it could be seen as a statement against erasure and oblivion. As notable American poet Jack Gilbert wrote, "Love lasts by not lasting."

At first, I'd planned on making it a sonnet, but the poem overflowed the 14-line constraint. There still might remain a sonnet-like feel underneath the poem, in its rhythm, flow and sensibility.

Wild and Unwieldy

What would the world be, once bereft
Of wet and of wildness? Let them be left,
O let them be left, wildness and wet;
Long live the weeds and the wilderness yet.
– Gerard Manley Hopkins ("Inversnaid")

In ditches on fringes by boulevard and berm
where green on the verge of descent meets gurgle
and rush draining downward and down
flowering the flow of sorrel, dandelion,
buttercup tease, their runners and taproots inching
in from the edges until we take up trowel and digger,
dig deeply and deeper, up by the roots
what the world would be. Once bereft

of thistle and burr, the prickle and burn of
the unwanted other, we'd miss them, rush off
with digger in hand to redefine wildflowers—
from ditch and berm we'd fetch them,
bring back to our gardens and hearts in the concrete
wilderness what we long to control but can't
though we cultivate and cull, shovel and shove. Let's
let them be left. O let them be left,

the toadflax and tansy, to decorate lots we'll leave
open for them; give foxtail its place
in sidewalks and patios to fill in the cracks
nobody mends; let hawkweed and henbit splatter
our streets with their feisty palette, a summer bouquet
over aquifers of a past still trickling beneath our feet
as we peer through barricades of rain in a mindset
of wet. And wildness. Wildness and wet

just past the back door, another bountiful feast
in brambles. Punctured and drenched, we stand
purpled and bursting with the plump and the luscious...
There are harvests larger than we're meant
to collect, like the wild and unwieldy thriving
in the midst of our densities to feed and protect
the feral and winged, their dens and their nests—
long live the weeds and the wilderness yet.

—⋙—

I wrote "Wild and Unwieldy" over several months in 2009–10 when I was still living in Vancouver. By then, I'd been there for almost four decades—but, raised in a small New Brunswick town, I never felt I fully belonged in an urban world. I suspect this is why many of my poems, one way or another, seek out what remains of nature in the city or hark back to my rural roots—and why, once it became possible to do so, I left Vancouver for Pender Island.

This particular poem was sparked by the intense push toward greater densification in the city and how so many people felt their voices were not being heard by planners, politicians and developers. Years ago, I'd added the Hopkins excerpt to my collection of favourite quotes, thinking it would make a good epigraph for a poem, or maybe a book. Then, in July 2009, when I found myself fretting yet again about how densification was proceeding, it occurred to me that these four lines could work as the beginning of a glosa addressing the issue—so I decided to give it a try.

Once I began writing, weeds became, for me, a metaphor for the disregarded. I found myself thinking, not just about densification per se, but about appreciation—how what we treasure can too often be dictated by what's "in" and what's "out," rather than by discovering the inherent value in something as simple as, say, a dandelion; about how we routinely apply the phrase "invasive species" to the overly aggressive in nature, yet rarely think to apply it to ourselves; for that matter, about the misguided concept of our species being above and separate from the rest of nature; about how we have such trouble getting the balance right...

PETER CULLEY

Five North Vancouver Trees

for Lary Bremmer

Here and there between the pages a skeleton leaf conjured up
those lost woods — Patrick Leigh Fermor

I.

The phylogeny of sleep
vs. the ontogeny of waking up

bunnybeard blankets
dewdrop the sleeping slutswool

drooled voices skitter
from the back of a tent (circus)

useless user fingers pinch
filched bodega grapes

awake in sheets so soft
you devour them in a dream

goose feathers knuckle
a wet November no-hitter's

bloody stucco,
horseradish breezes

curl brown paint from gray lumber
in soft curls—

an August half-moon
teething at sixes & sevens,

in sheets so soft they squeezed
phantom pain out of real pain,

excuses thumbed a map's wet fold,
a ghost train fringe marked with

misty rivers, chenille fingers, flutter gulches,
cross-digging legends out of anthracite

shaded parks bunted for cornerboys
that flap & tumble & shamble.

"Five North Vancouver Trees" was written for the "Moodyville" issue of *The Capilano Review*, a celebration/examination of North Vancouver, where the magazine is published, "Moodyville" being an old term for the municipality. I'm not sure why I was asked to participate, but for some reason I took the assignment seriously and endeavoured to produce something about North Vancouver that could still somehow fit in with *Hammertown*, my hometown Nanaimo mock-epic. As a spur, I asked if my photographs could be used, and was told that I could have five black-and-white images. I was then beginning to take a lot of photographs, especially of trees, so one cool spring day I took the ferry over, and instead of taking the blue bus straight through to Vancouver spent a morning wandering around North Vancouver taking pictures of trees for *The Capilano Review*.

The images were no great shakes, but wandering around North Vancouver was generative, its long hills, sudden parks and time-capsule cafés made for a good morning's walk. Dedicating the poem was easy, as Lary Bremner, then living in Japan, was the only born and bred North Vancouverite I knew, and at worst the poem might be a reminder of his home. The writing of the poem happened, after all the preparations, very quickly. What led to any given line or word combination I can't really say, but some experiences I had fed into it. The most time I had ever spent in North Vancouver was as a teenage poet in the late '70s, when I fell in with some poets who lived there and became a kind of mascot for a few months, a mixed experience. But the one memory I can see all through the poem happened more recently. Coming into North Vancouver to attend an opening at Presentation House Gallery I got on the wrong blue bus and instead of travelling ten minutes from Park Royal to the gallery the bus kept going uphill for a long, dreamlike time, and the thick hedges and dim lights of those misty upper reaches stuck in my mind. North Vancouver had always been a mysterious, dark place to me, and the poem works if it gets some of that over, folding into the larger narratives of *Hammertown* without too much strain. When getting the poem ready for book publication I realized the photographs weren't necessary beyond their occasion.

Kerrisdale

The real estate ad reads:
Elevate Yourself to Kerrisdale.

See them venturing
down these clean streets, the careful

steps of the elderly; their eyes,
their blue trembling hands.

Who knows where they have been,
what they have seen?

Whole families erased.
Like tables stripped of their settings.

They visit the coffee shops, the deli
for shavings of meat and cheese.

Turn shoes over
for the price on the sole.

(*Away melancholy,*
Away with it, let it go).

And you with your hot, raw heart.
You too wear widow's black;

scrape your hair back off your
white face, your red-rimmed eyes.

Perhaps lipstick:
British Red.

—ɷ—

I wrote this after I had left someone whom I loved, but couldn't live with. I moved briefly to an apartment in Kerrisdale. I felt uprooted and strange in this new neighbourhood. Lots of the people around me were elderly women, and watching them shopping I thought about their lives and losses. The snobbish real estate ad "Elevate Yourself to Kerrisdale" was around at that time and I found it rather ironic. The white face / red lipstick image seems ghoulish, and is also a nod to my English heritage. The spare couplets reflect the "careful steps" and the focus on small details. The quote is from Stevie Smith's poem "Away Melancholy"—she was plucky, and one of the first poets I read. I suppose it is a poem about grief, resilience, and the masks we wear.

Just after 11 on Remembrance Day

The man in the red hoodie
Un-stemmed against the *No Stopping* sign
In the middle of Clarkson Street

Is being questioned by two police
Towering in their power-stances over him
While he explains what it is like

To have nothing but a rough green
Duffel bag and the desire only to sleep,
A bead of blood hunched against

November, and as they endlessly interrogate
His unaddressed presence, a cross of bomber
Planes pass, twice, over the river, with their trembling

Engines, and now I see his hair is silver, that the cops
Have moved beyond him, that the pavement is still
Bright with his sitting. What, in our darkness,

Are we waiting for.

—〰—

Living in downtown New Westminster, I witness a regular stream of often male homeless people travelling down the alleyway behind my apartment, usually on the quest for bottles or discarded consumer items. The man I wrote about in this poem, however, was just crouching on the corner for hours, not shooting up, not even sleeping, just hunched there. And yet, he was told to move, a man who may have been (his silver hair) one of the veterans we were supposedly commemorating that day. I loathe the war mentality, hierarchies of thoughtlessness, judgments against those who have never been fully integrated within the lie of the market economy or who have fallen away from security due to mental illness, poverty, or other hardships. So there is message here but mostly there is noticing, which is what poems can do well, see the red hoodie, the green duffel bag, the trembling engines (and sound at the core of seeing). Then ask the question, why is justice taking so long?

I write something every day I get to sit and watch beyond myself, whether it's the river, or human passersby, or birds. The morning is the most exquisite time for words. If there is silence. Coffee. Reading poetry then, waiting. I want a collusion of rhythms to draw the unknowingness from me, form a flowing that at its peak serves up that "surprise for the writer" that Frost claimed was essential to producing an equivalent shiver in the reader. The reader, that mysterious being. Almost, the poem itself, its own eyes, mind, scanning the lines, whispering again (is it?), yes.

fresh ancient ground

"Since 1978, over 14 billion dollars
have been taken out of our traditional territory.
Yet my family still goes without running water."
– Melina Laboucan Massimo, Lubicon Cree woman

"When you can't trust the water, it's terrifying"
– James Cameron visiting the Tar Sands

can the water trust us?

chasing temporary jobs that evaporate
like so much acid rain drifting into Saskatchewan

"overburden removal" leaves poisonous polycyclic aromatic hydrocarbons, pah.
the PAHs stink. swallow them and die a slow cancerous death

those who don't respect the magic of ice
are doomed to melt it for their descendants

as miles of living medicines made by rivers over millennia
are unceremoniously eradicated, annihilated, wasted

everything leaking everywhere it wasn't meant to go
rainbow in the sky or on slick oil

held captive by toxic water, undrinkable yet thinkable,
blistering fish inside out, thirsty children sickened

caribou killed by omnibus rampage, eliminating water
from legislation in the federal abdication of responsibility

what is the language of decay, & how can we not afford to learn that dialect?
350, 398, 400, 450, as the outer count changes the inner one

we walk for healing the scar sands, in a living pact with the bears, the eagles,
the muzzled scientists, the beavers who've built dams you can see from outer space

step by step, we conduct ceremony for those who don't know any better or don't
    care, broken
whole, waiting for our sisters & brothers to catch up with wind, sun & water

—ᴍ—

From 2010 to 2013, I committed to participate in the healing walk for the tar sands, as well as a fifth year helping to organize a solidarity healing walk in Montreal. I have no words big enough for the horror I feel when I see and smell the tar sands. Bearing witness to the devastation is one of the hardest things I have ever done. Alone, I would have curled into a fetal ball and sobbed for what has been lost and destroyed. Even now, when I think about the land up north, let myself feel the everyday brutality that has been normalized through massive industry, my throat stops and my eyes fill with tears. In the company of the healing walkers, led by indomitable Cree and Dene elders and everyday people, determined Keepers of the Athabasca, mothers, fathers, aunties, uncles, concerned citizens, we reassert human responsibilities to land, water, life.

These responsibilities can be fostered or ignored by the cultures we are raised in, but the responsibilities and relationships remain regardless of how we are socialized. They are embedded in each breath we take, each sip of water we swallow, each bite of food provided by the land, no matter how much humans manipulate, redirect, reshape or try to control what the earth provides.

Whether or not we were taught these responsibilities by our families and education systems, we can still learn how to address them. We can remember that dignity and meaning comes from keeping the earth healthy for future generations for all living creatures, plants and animals, not just humans. We can look frankly at what is not going well—the destruction of natural habitat, the dangers posed by global warming, the inequities and violence in our own cultures—and do better. We are capable of it, if we care to try.

* * *

When I asked Melina about quoting her for the epigraph of this poem, she wrote back, "I would be more inclined to talk about the sacredness and contamination of the water as opposed to focusing on the money being made since the land is priceless." Yes. A huge, life-affirming YES.

As a postscript to this poem, I would like to quote Melina once more: "There are solutions... We need to shift away from fossil-fuel based systems and push for a renewable energy system that can help us transition out of what we are currently facing."

GEORGE STANLEY

The Vacuum Cleaner

I'd almost finished the vacuuming
when the on-off switch (that had been wonky for months)
finally broke. I couldn't turn the machine off,
it was stuck on on. So I finished vacuuming
& unplugged it. Next week I took it in to the shop.

A beautiful girl
came out from in back.
I handed her the vacuum cleaner
(the power head, that is;
the attachments I'd left at home),
and as she inspected it, we began to talk
in a friendly way—about what
I don't remember, but I recall feeling
that I was not just a customer
to her.

The beauty of girls
and boys
pursues me
wherever I'm going.

Then I had to take my head in—to the clinic.
I sat in the examining room
waiting for the door to open.
Then it did. The young doctor
entered & said, "I'm Jason."

I think the poem clicks when the "I" takes his head in—to the clinic. For a second, there's the ludicrous image of a man *carrying* his head, as he had carried the power head of the vacuum cleaner into the repair shop. I was working on both ends of the poem at the same time. I needed to come up with some concise way of expressing the fact that it wasn't the entire vacuum cleaner, with its hose, suction units, and wheeled base, but only—the phrase came to me—"the power head." (Indeed, coming up with this phrase recapitulated what I had to do when I decided to take the vacuum cleaner in—to strip it of its attachments.)

When it became clear to me that "power head" was the right term for the vacuum cleaner as I handed it to the girl, simultaneously the right phrase for the reason why I was attending the clinic also came to me—"to take my head in." The poem clicked—it came to life.

"The Vacuum Cleaner" is an "objectivist" poem about ordinary life in the city. Three locations: an apartment, a vacuum cleaner repair shop, a community medical clinic. The figures who appear, after the "I," are the girl, whose way of speaking is friendly, and the young doctor, who introduces himself in a friendly way, as "Jason" (rather than as Dr. So-and-so). The poem is, then, a tribute to friendliness.

There are two specific lines I would call attention to. It took me much pondering and rejecting roundabout phrasings, before I arrived at the perfectly idiomatic "came out from in back." And note that it's not "wherever I go," which might just refer to the paths the "I" takes as he travels about the city; but the more weighty "wherever I'm going," which might continue, "in this life."

GEORGE BOWERING

I Like Summer

I like summer so much,
the way the tiniest rock gets a shadow behind it,
the kind of shadow that makes Mars photographs so interesting,
the rocks and shadows you never thought of
when you were a boy imagining a voyage to Mars
or other planets you preferred
because the general run of boys your age were Mars fans
the way they were Roy Rogers fans so you were a Gene Autry fan,
and a Red Sox fan because they knew no better than
to favour the New York Yankees, and that continues
so that now young women visiting from Japan
wear pink hats with white New York Yankees insignia
and their boyfriends have their hair dyed blond,
but that doesn't really work because Japanese hair
seems to go orange when you dye it, which is fashion,
isn't it? You have to hand it to someone
who makes an asset out of what looks like a drawback,
hence the invention of scrapple, which I tasted for the first time
at the Florida Avenue Grill in Washington, D.C., having always
wondered what Charlie Parker and Diz were talking about
that winter's night in 1947.

I have been asked to write a few words about my poem "I Like Summer," wherein I should speak to "behind the poem" as well as what I was writing toward, what the influence was, the context or background, and the impetus or spark. I'm sorry to start this so clumsily, but I feel that I have to say something about the difficulty I have in trying to see a relationship between my writing and these notions.

I simply can't tell you anything about what is or was "behind the poem." I know that some teachers used to like to discuss the idea behind the poem or the feeling behind the poem. But honestly, when I am sitting there, pen connecting me with the page, I don't see or imagine anything behind the poem. I am not looking through or around the poem to see something. I don't see any "background"; the poem is immediately present, and any part of it is related not to something elsewhere, but something that is also happening in the poem. Hence rime, for example.

So the only thing I was "writing toward" was the right margin, or the end of the poem. The poem, said Philip Whalen, is a graph of a mind moving. If this poem was influenced by any specific poet, that would be John Ashbery, whose poems I have been buying since the sixties, and whose work I have been reading in the mornings a lot lately. Yes, I might have been writing like Ashbery, but I think that I do it with a lot more attention to sound. Tone-leading of the vowels, a poet once said.

So a lot of my recent poems start with a line that found its way into and through my head: "I like summer so much," for example. Another might have been "I used to wonder what old guys were thinking." Some time later, when I feel the buzz, I will return to the poem and keep adding lines until it is over. "I like Summer" found its way back, and what a pleasure it is when that happens. And honest to god, I didn't notice till now that the first and last lines are similarly short, and thus have an authority that is the poem's.

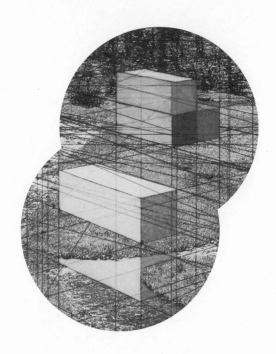

RACHEL ROSE

Golden Age

This one is for the girls
who got themselves to the party
and didn't get home, girls
who got drunk like angels—glimmering,
disappearing—then woke up under a towel
in a strange hotel. This is the glass of words to toast
your bad choices, the wink of a boy
tonguing your navel. Unconscious-
ly your own desire to be touched
was a claim you couldn't stake, a willow
that needed water. This is the blame you've birthed,
cradled and nursed, blame that won't leave home
because you didn't bite, didn't sit up, you just
closed your eyes and drifted on a sad river of burning
alcohol. This is for all the passive girls, the ones who sucked off
popular boys, the ones who half-wanted to be wanted,
half wanted to die. To die a little death
as you did then, when you came to school
and the rumour was he'd fucked you with the handle
of a broom while you were floating down
the Ganges, the Nile, the Fraser, the Thames.
Gone: was it true or wasn't it? There was no pain,
it was a lie, it was a myth. This is for you,
bitch, snatch of gossip in the hall,
twist of hair, sucker punch. This is for me, too:
girl of the skinned knees who couldn't name the names
of those who'd passed through her body.
This is for leaving school, or staying. For the dangerous
damaged pack we make, the way we smell blood
where other girls smell roses. Sinister sorority!
Who knew that one day we would consider
ourselves lucky to have been raped
in the golden age of rape, before violation
was caught on an iPhone: posted, reposted. Look!
A close-up on sleeping beauty digitally defiled
and then digitally defiled. What poisoned apple

blocks her throat from screaming? Boots jostle. Time fucks
faster now. Featherweight, angelweight, song of floating
above the below. Blow and she's still still: moth dust, shimmer.
Unbuckle your belt, her eyelids. She can't move away,
can't change schools. Even dead, there is
no escape. Link it. Click like. It takes three thousand views
in three hours to make a myth.

I think the poem contains its own reflection. That is, I think the context and background of violence against women throughout the ages and how that violence has shifted in the digital age is the heart of the poem, and I wrote it to change people's hearts.

My poem is not subtle, and, as I tend to do in a lot of my work, I use irony as a means of communication of the hardest subjects. Irony is often my preference as a way of telling the truth, but telling it slant (to paraphrase Emily Dickinson).

RAY HSU

Narrator

The notion of creativity must be broadly used, not just to refer to the produc-tion of a new artistic object or form, but to problem solving in every imaginable field. Far from being germane to the arts alone, creativity is vital to industry and business, to educate and to social and community development.
— The World Commission on Culture and Development, UNESCO

The lone and level sands stretch far away.
— Percy Bysshe Shelley, "Ozymandias"

To ease the guilt of going on an empire tells a story of its merchants to give itself some vast shape, an overarching idea. Travelling court to court one hears stories of imports and notable exports, creating their own universes drawn neither from the future nor from the classics. Despite best efforts, they entertain: despite them-selves, imagination lurks in secret folds. Wealth makes our city liveable.

There are no pedestrians. Those who step out are fair game for enthusiastic traffic. Daily life, no matter what it is built on, they say, can be fuelled by superlative: witness the tallest tower / the richest horse race / the world's ...

It is hard not to be impressed. The mind does not know where to start: architec-ture or its souvenir afterlife. They say the planners are looking. They say an under-class does the dirty work and lives and works somewhere in the neighbourhood. Some say this a street-level affair that couldn't be further away from an empire that just a blink ago had no history, no ancient encumbrances. But new scores require settling. One grassy verge will remain, vivid beneath the visiting workers who meet over lunch in the passing day's light.

—⚬—

(Ancient Play, a Masque)

Chain gang, a chorus of prisoners.
Pedestrian, an ancient-looking man.
Tourism, a greying paint splash.

Chain gang: An empire tells a story
(beat)
to ease the guilt of going on.
(beat)
Far and wide, its merchants
(beat)
fling a story: some vast shape
(beat)
some overarching idea.
(beat)
An empire tells a story
(beat)
Traveling from court to court
(beat)
one hears stories.
(beat)
Imports
(beat)
notable exports.
                    / An empire tells a story /
/ An empire tells a story /
                              / to ease the guilt of going on /
to find a figure that speaks
(beat)
for me.

Pedestrian: What are you saying?
Is this the future? Or some classic?
Or some entertainment? Despite
what you say, I sense in your secret language

imagination. I hear few superlatives
and that makes me suspicious.

Tourism: Actually, I find this
impressive. My mind doesn't know where to start,
it's so much. Do I look
or wish for a souvenir? Somewhere in the neighbourhood
are workers. I hear they live around here.

Chain gang: Only a blink ago
(beat)
this empire had no history no scores
(beat)
to settle
(beat)
but now you can glimpse
(beat)
a vivid patch
(beat)
of green beneath
(beat)
(beat)
it all.

PRAYER

LET THE SKY ESCAPE
  LET THE SKY ESCAPE
    LET THE SKY ESCAPE
      LET THE SKY ESCAPE AT LEAST
AT LEAST LET THE SKY ESCAPE PLEASE AT LEAST
        LET THE SKY ESCAPE

YOUR CARS YOUR BOATS YOUR FLYING THINGS
YOUR WATERSKIS YOUR BASEBALL BATS YOUR ORANGE WIGS
YOUR DREAMS OF THE FUTURE YOUR LATE-NIGHT TALK SHOWS
YOUR GATHERINGS OF CLOSE FRIENDS YOUR WHISPERED REMINISCENCES
YOUR MOMENTS OF SURRENDER YOUR LAST MOMENT
OF UNCONDITIONAL LOVE

LET THE SKY ESCAPE
  LET THE SKY ESCAPE
    LET THE SKY ESCAPE
      LET THE SKY ESCAPE AT LEAST
AT LEAST LET THE SKY ESCAPE PLEASE AT LEAST
        LET THE SKY ESCAPE

YOUR SEMI-ECSTATIC REFLECTIONS YOUR ELEGANT POWDERED NOSE
YOUR CASUAL WALK TO THE DOOR YOUR REAL FEELINGS
ALL THE THINGS YOU REALLY WANT TO DO
YOUR UNCOMPLETED MISSIONS
YOUR SLIM CHANCES AND YOUR FAT ONES THE WORLD AS WE SEE IT
WHENEVER YOU GET THE CHANCE AND HOWEVER IT HAPPENS

LET THE SKY ESCAPE
  LET THE SKY ESCAPE
    LET THE SKY ESCAPE
      LET THE SKY ESCAPE AT LEAST
AT LEAST LET THE SKY ESCAPE PLEASE AT LEAST
        LET THE SKY ESCAPE

YOUR FOLDED HOURS YOUR NURSING SIBLINGS
THE HEAT OF YOUR BLOOD YOUR EXQUISITE ESCAPES

YOUR QUICK ENTRECHATS YOUR SYSTEMATIC DYSLEXIA
YOUR SWEET AND EASY FORGETFULNESS YOUR RARE
UNGUARDED MOMENTS YOUR SLOW FUCKS
AND YOUR QUICK ONES WHATEVER YOU CAN GET

LET THE SKY ESCAPE
  LET THE SKY ESCAPE
    LET THE SKY ESCAPE
AT LEAST LET THE SKY ESCAPE PLEASE AT LEAST
      LET THE SKY ESCAPE

YOUR CONDITIONED FREEDOM YOUR HOUSE AND GARDEN
YOUR READY REMARKS YOUR CLOSE ACQUAINTANCESHIP
YOUR QUAINT BUT UNFORGETTABLE HABITS
YOUR GLACIAL CALM AND YOUR QUICK ANGER
WHATEVER IT IS THAT MAKES US FORGET YOU
YOU AND YOUR NEWLY ELECTED PRESIDENTS AND PRIME MINISTERS

LET THE SKY ESCAPE
  LET THE SKY ESCAPE
    LET THE SKY ESCAPE
      LET THE SKY ESCAPE AT LEAST
AT LEAST LET THE SKY ESCAPE PLEASE AT LEAST
      LET THE SKY ESCAPE

YOUR LONGING LOOKS YOUR IMPENETRABLE EMOTION
YOUR HIDDEN MEANINGS YOUR LOST INNOCENCE
YOUR SLY GLANCES YOUR PERFIDIOUS ENCOUNTERS
YOUR OPAQUE MOMENTS AND YOUR TRANSPARENT ONES
YOUR APPARENT READINESS YOUR IMPURE THOUGHTS
YOUR MOMENTS OF SUDDEN RECOGNITION YOUR PURE EPIPHANIES

LET THE SKY ESCAPE
  LET THE SKY ESCAPE
    LET THE SKY ESCAPE
AT LEAST LET THE SKY ESCAPE PLEASE AT LEAST
      LET THE SKY ESCAPE

YOUR SMART BOMBS AND YOUR STUPID HUMAN BEINGS
YOUR CATEGORICAL IMPERATIVES YOUR STANDARDS
OF OBJECTIVE TRUTH YOUR NECESSARY JUDGEMENTS
YOUR RESPONSIBLE LEADERSHIP YOUR WELCOME TAX CUTS
YOUR LITTLE LUXURIES YOUR KID'S CANDY
YOUR BABY'S DESIREFUL WAILINGS WHATEVER IT IS
THAT YOU ARE WAITING FOR

LET THE SKY ESCAPE
 LET THE SKY ESCAPE
  LET THE SKY ESCAPE
   LET THE SKY ESCAPE AT LEAST
AT LEAST LET THE SKY ESCAPE PLEASE AT LEAST
    LET THE SKY ESCAPE

"Prayer" is really a political rant rather than a poem or a prayer. The prayerful element in the piece is the repeated refrain of "LET THE SKY ESCAPE," addressed to unnamed powers of the earth. My poems are usually meant to be read aloud in order to allow readers to appreciate the music of their composition mellifluous or cacophonic. They are nevertheless mostly the works of a literary page poet, whispered fervently and intimately into the hopefully receptive and reflective readers' ears. "Prayer," by contrast, was deliberately written as a noisy boisterous performance piece, the score or script for a single or several mingled voices.

I wanted the direct and physical connection to a living audience that only public performance allows. I worked in admiring imitation of the tradition of outstanding Vancouver poets bill bissett and billy little, as well as some earlier modernist practitioners of the ranting political style, notably Allen Ginsberg and the 1930s American self-described proletarian poet, Kenneth Fearing. The poem is written through what I call a "semi-automatic" method, to distinguish it both from the fully automatic early style of the surrealists and the more rigorously composed style of other modern poets.

The sky, which irrevocably needs to be allowed to escape, was conceived as the space of human freedom and imagination, insanely threatened by the militarization of space itself in the form of the "Star Wars" program of Ronald Reagan. The rant is simply a freely associated list of some of the trivializing objects, clichés and pieties of North American consumer culture, tossed into the air as if by an explosion of words…with any luck, a means to break free from the deadening concepts of the culture which reflects the economics and politics of the times.

how it is (November 2007)

MAIN

Owl Drugs

no-name money mart

Hotel Washington

convenience store

empty building

the Balmoral

pizza shop

porn store

Insite (North America's 1st legal
safe injection site)

Vancouver Drug School (call the whole damn
neighbourhood the Vancity Drug School)

empty lot

empty building (the old Smilin' Buddha
where my dad saw Jimi Hendrix)

art gallery

subsidized housing project

COLUMBIA

MAIN

the heart of the community

the Roosevelt

convenience store

the Regent

closed business

closed business

closed business

closed business

the Blue Eagle

the Brandiz

closed business

convenience store

convenience store

COLUMBIA

how it is (January 2012)

MAIN	MAIN
Owl Drugs	the heart of the community
no-name money mart	the Roosevelt
Hotel Washington	convenience store
convenience store	the Regent
empty building	dev. app. no. DE414810
the Balmoral	dev. app. no. DE414810
pizza shop	dev. app. no. DE414810
porn store	dev. app. no. DE414810
Insite (North America's 1st legal safe injection site)	dev. app. no. DE414810
Art gallery	the Brandiz
community garden instead of social housing	art gallery
empty building (the old Smilin' Buddha where my dad saw Jimi Hendrix)	convenience store
art gallery	convenience store
subsidized housing project	COLUMBIA
COLUMBIA	

how it is (November 2014)

MAIN

Owl Drugs

no-name money mart

Maple Hotel PPP Canada SRO Initiative

convenience store

empty building

the Balmoral

pizza shop

closed porn store

Insite (North America's 1st legal
safe injection site)

art gallery

community garden instead of social housing

empty building (the old Smilin' Buddha
where my dad saw Jimi Hendrix)

art gallery

subsidized housing project

COLUMBIA

MAIN

the heart of the community

the Roosevelt

convenience store

the Regent

dev. app. no. DE414810 approved

—79 units of market housing

—9 units of 'affordable' housing

—9 units at welfare shelter rate

dev. app. no. DE414810 approved

the Brandiz

art gallery

convenience store

convenience store

COLUMBIA

I started mapping the Downtown Eastside after reading Robert Fitterman's "Metropolis 16." The iteration I read was composed of short lists of spaces of consumption, which are repeated in various order over several pages—places like KFC, The Gap, McDonald's, Walmart, Kmart. Immediately I thought of lone and lonely commuters driving their cars through vast, homogenized and ever-sprawling suburban spaces. I noticed a similar repetition of certain spaces of consumption in the Downtown Eastside, though on a much smaller scale of a few city blocks. Deteriorating hotels where Vancouver's poor take shelter in substandard housing, overpriced "convenience" stores, closed businesses, and empty lots abounded. But then the neighbourhood began to change, to be "revitalized," and I began to represent the gentrification of the Downtown Eastside. I didn't realize then I would map how it is again and again, yet as the fight over some of the most valuable real estate in the nation continues, so too does the poem.

WANDA JOHN-KEHEWIN

Chai Tea Rant

Last night I went for a drive for about two hours. I thought I better not fill up again, so I put in the last $10 $1 bill I had in my wallet before the gas prices go up again. I went driving over the bridge, under the other bridge, around the bridge, and away around the other bridge, under a large chai tea. All the Tim Hortons with my $1.64 and said to myself, "Heck yeah! I'm at least worth a drive for about two hours." I figured I may as well or carelessly put together, depending on the tears of sadness and whatever purpose there was supposed to be, someone's babe, yeah. All the while playing a CD I made and titled "Babe's Sad Songs." (I figured I may as well be someone's babe ...) I listened to all these songs physically and sang along to John Waite's "I ain't missing you at all," and those here only in spirit. Shania Twain sang "Black eyes ... / Blue tears give me freedom." Then Sheryl Crow and The Dixie Chicks sang "Would you be man enough to be my man?" and out came the tears of sadness, and I understood because sometimes I just want to pick myself up at the bottom of the gutter and trek back up and face the people on my cell call list and told them I loved them, getting my phone cut off in the process—then I would have pulled out my $1.64 and got a chai tea by walking through the drive thru ...

And I thought about my dad's funeral—this was the song, because of how we tried to control each other. The song he wanted, relationship deconstruction, and figured I wasn't angry anymore; only sad to realize that they were also very angry. "Would you be man enough to be my man?" ... R.E.M.'s "Everybody Hurts." He used to play that song after that was in wine at his funeral. He used to go off the deep end like my mother once again, and face my harshest critic in the mirror once again and pull ...

"Everybody Hurts," and I cried and as the tears blurred my view of the road, a recovering alcoholic; he kept blood-coloured red. I thought of all the failed, broken, hurtful relationships. In the next song, staining my purse, knocked out my smoke-stained little mouth a deep, almost abused, broken. And thought to myself, "I must be still worth a $1.64 ..." I lost my pocket, staining my purse; I would have lost this time my $1.64.

I veered back into my own lane and marvelled at different strategies and one-on-one individualized relationship. Then I think that I'd only have to quit close to twenty-five years or so. I found blood-coloured red, a psychic healer's card in my bra, called all the people ... "I must be still worth a $1.64 ..."

When my son was seven, I wrote this poem. Age seven was when I was in a foster home and suffered different abuses, so when my son turned seven, I felt this deep sadness. I looked at him, his innocence, his trust and couldn't imagine how anyone could intentionally hurt a seven-year-old. The effects of colonization run deep into my background and colour the edges of my writing. I am healing day by day, year by year and write about such sensitive topics to perhaps help others through their silence. I write about these sensitive things when I have processed them and put them on their proper shelf within my being. They are a part of me but do not define me. They allow me to reach beyond human condition and "stand in my truth" and share my experiences to educate others in a creative way.

REG JOHANSON

1) Then I wake up / Wrong city / Confronted with loneliness   /

Symptom of the sovereign's freedom

2) ***There's no ideal form of action. What's essential is that action assume a certain form, that it give rise to a form instead of having one imposed on it.***

Form imposes homeostasis / Balances, pauses / Renders recognizable / Enters history

/ Gives marching orders / The housing and services / Due the poor citizen

3) Upriver / Hope has turned to snow / — Crossroads — /

Highway 5, 3, or 1 / Kamloops / Nelson / Cache Creek /

Coquihalla / Rogers / Crowsnest /

Pass, treacherous / Dangerous Alberta

4) Flesh, language / We are together / In various forms / Nostalgic or hopeful /

Temporary or enduring / Tossing and turning / All night / Never enough / Is that /

All there is / What would it be like / Was there enough, once? / Could there be /

Enough / In the future / If we did things differently? /

How do we subsist?

Form of the difference / Form of the future

5) Giving form to, historicizing, socializing / Turning power / (*potencia*) / Into power

(poder) / Then rendered uninhabitable by / Critique (experience) / Then the

reactionary / Or negative—not negating— / Heroics of addiction / Living a civil war

between a / Minority faction, the angels of death / And a stronger majority of / Able

citizens / Or? / The spaces of negation / The Zomia[1] / The other side of the fence /

The camps / Here "poet" means something else

6) Because the centre isn't empty / There's a city there / Of the dead /

With history / Records / Libraries / Many selves / Real / If not true /

To each other / Encamped / Agreed to even if only by / Inertia /

The physical plant of love / Against which we postulate / An elsewhere /

An outside / Basic, useful

The poem began in thinking about form—form in art, in political struggle, and in spirituality. I was thinking about change. I experience the fact of the impermanence of things as a beautiful liberation (things change, thank god!), but I also fear loss; I struggle to change things, but also to preserve them. This is the conundrum I was interested in. There are artistic, political, and spiritual stakes in flux.

A figure of this conundrum is the zombie, the "living dead." And living-dead is a good description of my experience of drug and alcohol addiction, which has been definitive for me. To live again I needed to change.

As many have pointed out (i.e. Stevphen Shukaitis, *Imaginal Machines: Autonomy and Self-Organization in Revolutions of Everyday Life*) life under capitalism is zombie-life: any form-of-life that can't or won't be subsumed by capital is driven to extinction. As the forces of capital zombify the urban spaces of Vancouver, a civil war opens up. My poem asks, what is the form of the difference we seek to live?

Artistically, I am always impressed by artists who (appear to) think formally first that is, they are interested in formal questions to begin with. I think of this as a "top down" approach. I think of my own approach as "bottom-up"—I'm responding to an urgency that doesn't present itself in formal terms. Form comes later. Form-aldehyde. But like the Invisible Committee says: "It is crucial that action assume a certain form." Form = identity. A trap. A "box." But also agency.

This is also Nietzsche's distinction between Apollo and Dionysus: Apollo gives form to the formless *potencia* of Dionysus. Apollo is visual art, Dionysus is music. That's why there are so many allusions to music in the poem, especially to the blues.

---

[1] From James Scott, *The Art of Not Being Governed*: "The signal, distinguishing trait of Zomia, vis-à-vis the lowland regions it borders, is that it is relatively stateless [...] Zomia is [...] a region of refuge as well. By 'refuge,' I mean to imply that much of the population in the hills has, for more than a millennium and a half, come there to evade the manifold afflictions of state-making projects in the valleys" (19, 23).

The Place of Scraps concludes with a series of images that oscillate between Marius Barbeau's anthropological documentations and a photographic account of the poet's interaction with the totem poles in Vancouver. There is a conscious interplay between past and present, text and image, orientation and disorientation. The scraps of erasures from the previous sections of the book seem to appear without context. Where are the original documents that are being erased? What is leftover from the incomplete erasures?

All of the images that seemed to be so orderly and extraneous in earlier sections of *The Place of Scraps* are no longer confined to the space between poems but are now the content of the poems themselves. All the scraps and detritus of previous erasures are no longer positioned in proximity to a source but are at the height of visibility. The poet and Barbeau appear together here. Temporality is flattened out through the position of the author as photographer. Where does Barbeau begin? Where does Barbeau end? Where does the poet begin? Where does the poet end? Where does text begin? Where does text end?

In this moment, the poet finds himself in Stanley Park. There are poles; there are people. What function do these poles have? What roles are these people playing? How do they interact with each other? Is Barbeau present in this photo? Is the poet present in this photo? The city is certainly here. Is there a spatial relationship between the vertical heft of the skyscrapers and the totem poles? Are these poles here simply as a tourist attraction? As pieces of art to be taken in by cyclists? Are the poles bound by text? Drenched in broken-down, half-remembered stories? Are we looking at these poles from the right angle?

12 AM   12 PM

sweden   switzerland

windward   leeward

winnipeg   windsor

bow stern   port starboard

austria   australia

downstream   upstream

iran   iraq

recto   verso

guyanna   guiana

bd nu   mw pq

costa rica   puerto rico

next   previous

genoa   geneva

longitude   latitude

slovenia   slavonia

rosencrantz   guildenstern

vimy   vichy

astrology   astronomy

eminent   imminent

the other right   the other left

centripetal   centrifugal

My poem assembles words that are frequently confused, be it in other peoples' lexicons or in my own. Pairs like "automatic" and "autonomous" or "continuous" and "continual." Or one that I have never been able to nail down: "Winnipeg" and "Windsor." Of course, I know Winnipeg and Windsor are very different cities that are widely separated. I have close friends in both places. But my brain often produces the wrong name when I want to refer to one or the other. Curious, I gradually collected other such pairs, without any predetermined intent. As it turns out, many of the pairs I found refer to space, place or direction.

As a poem it may therefore be read as mimicking, remembering—and perhaps inducing—some of the stimulus-overload and social bewilderment that for people (like myself) raised in low population-density settings, is often an ongoing part of urban experience. Yet the piece also returns, as I often do in my writing, to the spare form of the carefully cultivated and carefully arranged (but non-exhaustive) list. In that capacity, it is presented as a resource. Think of it as a little corpus of mental glitch-inducing pairs that you could take up and use in your own work. In such poems-as-lists (or lists-as-poems), I want to draw attention to phenomena without overly directing what conclusions (or feelings or connections or information) a reader should draw. It's research.

riff what ought?

puddle kicker
parrot in the middle of a pumpkin patch / match-not-mate
PERFECT tragedy
BOOM they are killing us, all
the little messiahs
kick, bird, yr borne out fast

palate of pakistanis / the gothic jungle rumbling
with blue elephants
easily the lost hopi relatives of all arabs

when the clown wife is beaten
the women applaud

death wind comes early
on the open sea

facing a merciless city of painted ice
blue acidity of perverts and schemers

they think kindly of one another
when they're caught with their hand in the till

pear trees fall
a fa
la
la
la
fa
la

all my dreams of beauty flow
into the bath
my frail love falls on the road

he sings
in the street
some one
longs
for song

it's what's next the story reveals
pants falling down
or popping apart at the groin
sexual panic
relatives
pig-in-a-poke
the old joke
corks hanging from her hat
and feathers swinging on bead ropes
black and red medallions, popes' noses, newspaper strips sewn
all over

not against the wave
BE MERRY!
SWIM IN THE ARCTIC SEAS AND SHIVER INTENSELY
WITH THOSE YOU'VE GIVEN YRSELF TO

we can reach you in spite of yr fear
our bodies will need
your calm hand

"riff what ought?" is from a time when four or five friends would get together to transcend the thin strings of words to find a sound with our own particular music. Inside the small house east of Chinatown we'd haul out bamboo flutes and guitars and a small drum and, after smoking a small spliff and telling each other what we would, find a place to take off into another world.

Outside the window was a pear tree, an alley, many other small houses and beyond that the burgeoning virus of crammed glass towers that were soon to guarantee homelessness to citizens of Vancouver, old and young. And beyond that the sea rising to drown it all.

Poetry has been for me a transgressive transcendence; confession of faith or fault, the report of Emily Dickinson's loaded gun, of Rilke's horse, tethered on one leg, left out in a field, dancing for the god, Orpheus. I love to gather words, rub them together, feel them smell them taste them, find where they will take me. I love to twist syntax, watch a trope flare then fall into the rut of tales, climb little dream-cliffs; find myself the Muse's fool.

A poem is a string of words making rambling shapes full of spaces, lacunae, errors, excesses (ecstasy) that let you out of yourself to see the struggle between freedom and love.

I love to explore the politics of fellow animals, birds and snails, beggars and thieves.

A poem is a black stone, a white stone, a striped stone where everybody goes. Rivers run under our skin. I want it to never stop.

JORDAN SCOTT

Gate and glottal mount palate, drool the mollusc-husked haptic, glob clavicles chiffon. Its bruised mantle clatters the scarab musk, welts with, rill with, echoic aortas shunt long cyan divots diaphragms.

The pavilion is in the Coquitlam. The grass paces the wet of each day. The photographs of the pavilion, mouth aperture: one boy in the room, his gutturals click warm. The larynx is roomy. The flash cards, megamouth:

marbles mandible
slow tonic
phlegm Pango Pango
green's apples
tumble sea
mulch bumble
marble chunks
enamel smacks
tongue babble

Xerox bruise
onyx hues

Of my mouth and me. Of other people's fluent mouths and me. Of fluency and me. Of me and my mouth. Of me and other people's fluent mouths. Of me and fluency. My mouth and me. Fluent words and me. Other people's fluent mouths and me. Me and my mouth. Me and fluent. Me and other people's fluent mouths.

Therapy rooms in Coquitlam. Room mimics mouth; mouth mimics room. *Maintain natural eye contact refrain from filling in words don't give advice (e.g. relax, slow down) listen to what the person is saying rather than how they are saying it.* Upper Coquitlam; through a valley and up another hill. Recall the architecture of the room, stark and enormous, green and class angles, mint paint peeling. Recall the drive to the room: early and still warm from sleep. Birch shadows the basement. One body in a room; the line: *his gutturals click warm.* All the toys are puzzles. All whole rooms are beat boxes. And being approached by just ankles, large and swollen; and then the flashcards, enormous fluorescence. They do not fit in a mouth. Swallow is desire. Dysfluent carapace; duodenums wet with speech. *Cows, locomotives, ice cream and wolves.* And then the directions: what is this? Say this word. Say it. Say again. A poetics of kind of. Just the card in front of a face, taking up the whole room, blocking out vision and the outside. Just the word. The grit and guts—in mouth and on card. The game is to repeat; it's insistence, silly boy. And in repeating, a mouth is worn outside in weather. I once was a fabric or a laminate rectangle. I remember taking these cards home—stacks of them to practice. And I remember the decision, after trying them in the living room in October and it was cold. That I would not use them anymore.

un/authorized invocation

women of Prince George,
women of Vancouver,
women of Ciudad Juarez,
your long reach, a continent's bones—
    Anchorage to Prince Rupert,
    Vancouver to San Diego, and then inland—
Speak, women to N
absolve any heresy—
    is it, is it, is it, is it, is it
    wrong to—?
In the after-time the future accumulates forward and back—
    June 23, 1985.
This is British Columbia,
and of you, women of North America,
there is the not recorded, the not allowed:
your ecosphere where currents rise—
navigate to feel them, walk any road to sense—
It is June, 1985: unknowable presence that speaks—
Come, who murders,
who remains, in this life, in the next
in history, in the text made to be material,
and believe, and refuse to believe, the living, the dead
where is
    totality murdered, missing
    air   an entire coastline, stratosphere of suffering,
    with such force future
becomes past,
manifest in biosphere
dome to cover atrocities one to another—
this proposition arises from rock, from the shelf of mountains:
all murdered souls congregate
and speak. Speak, missing and murdered women
to N, to the children of Air India, atrocity to atrocity
a common language
opening passages in time
    and its dimensions, where messages may travel—

—※—

I wrote this poem in the middle of a five-year process, that of archive immersion, within the grief-work that was my sojourn inside a saga, the story of the bombing of Air India Flight 182, and its aftermath. During the writing of what would become a book-length sequence, and the first completed series of poems from my lifelong poem chronicle, *thecanadaproject*, what came to me, as in a rush of wind in a tunnel, was the need to seek supplication of the dead, those names released and unreleased. Who was I?—to transgress by writing about other people, the 329 passengers and crew that lost their lives on June 23, 1985, when their plane exploded over the Atlantic ocean, off the southern coast of Ireland. Eighty-two children under the age of 13 died in the bombing. My aunt and uncle, as well.

The writing of the poems taught me to bend low to documents, hundreds of them: testimonies, family records, court transcripts, news clippings, inquiry reports, and letters. From this material, located in a kind of stratosphere hovering above the text, rose the voices. Once they claimed me, (and of course I am shy about speaking of this, to do so risks cliché, and might even become a kind of sacrilege), then I needed not just guidance from the texts, but a sense of accompaniment.

To situate an act of mass murder, the loss of individual life, within a collective act of violence so virulent that it must perforce echo across time and space, well, that required contemplation: what does it mean to lose a child? What does it mean to lose, for instance, four generations of women in a single act of—dare we utter that most problematic of words, *terror*? It required ideology: what kind of poetic practice engages with the political, the social, from within language, acknowledging form and rhythm, cadence? And it required a kind of philosophical reckoning with the weight of history.

The more I read within the Air India/Canada archive, the more I saw how a bombing of a plane, arose not out of singularity, but as if from the ground-up, as part of a fabric of relations, those of Empire, its records, settlement, and intent. All of this led me to write a series within a series, of what I think of as *invocati*, an appeal of the poet to higher powers, to the spirit world, to the materiality of history, its dialectic, that atrocity speaks to atrocity. Dear reader, not any of these words can even approximate the sense of dread that enveloped me and does to this day, to take on the mantle of writing about murder. Perhaps at the core of any elegy, any lament, dirge, hymn, prayer, treatise, brief or document, is an unfathomable silence. What does it mean to kill another? What does it mean to bear the aftermath? We were speaking then of—

Of the Indexical, or, Hockey Night in the Anthropocene

And then we extend the climate
Of our unknowing

Despite false colour views and
Massive stacks of data

The moment wasn't about the
Symbolic after all

The moment followed a bee through
The streets of Manhattan

The earth spinning hot from its axis
Was—or wasn't—

More like a tree falling in a forest
Than it was like an instrument

Measuring CO_2 in Hawaii—
But if a tree falls in a forest

And everyone is already in that tree
Having climbed there

To get above rising waters
Does it make any sound?

Or is that just the noise our limbs make
Wind-milling in space

As we launch—indexical
Of our own distraction—

Off the ends of our
200-year-old hockey sticks?

Only one question remains: are we
Leaping away from each other

Or leaping towards the animals we
Always already knew we were?

—⊶—

I wrote this poem on the flight home from New York City, the day after joining 400,000 others in the People's Climate March (September 21, 2014). Most marchers were organized by group affiliation, and I marched with around 20 poets (many of whom had participated in a poetry and climate change workshop I had organized the day before). We were led by Cecilia Vicuña, carrying a wire and fabric bee atop a stick. It was more like a slow parade than anything else.

Writing about things like climate change is not easy—suffers from the problem of being just too big to see or grasp. "On the Indexical" appears to sweep up a few elements—Cecilia's bee wand, the idea of "hockey stick" graphs (those graphs of the past 200 or so years which show radical and exponential growth of almost everything—population, industrial production, carbon emissions, etc. etc.), and "false colour views" (those photographs and maps scientists use and artificially colour to accentuate what is actually hard to perceive). Then there is the old philosophical saw about the tree falling. Climate change is hard to conceive of because—we're all in the tree that's falling! This also gets at the main philosophical thrust of the poem: based on the idea of there being different forms of "signs," such as the indexical (a sort of pointing sign, almost universal in nature) and the symbolic (human language), it may be that climate change is difficult to deal with in language because it is largely an indexical event—a giant tree crashing, and now we have to interpret what *that* means (fight or flight?).

Ok—enough philosophy. I so often seem to write poems on planes. They come suddenly, after just catching the whiff of something. All peripheral vision. Hark, a poem approaches. Those first two lines as pure suggestion, pure overheard language, message from the Outside. Then the rest of the poem just comes along quickly as I listen and transcribe the collision of thoughts that have been rattling around inside me for several days. Now push on—the struggle continues.

south of the walls of the north
a poem for Angye Gaona & for her daughter

this small room and the child i swore to make a safe and
excellent world for, just for you, just for you and the me
that is touched and touched and touched by your small
saunterings

the big world mounting around us high and high as far as
eye can see, well beyond that, feel the weight of the waves
coming in to pummel this beach, my belly, this beach, my
this

belly of home, all across the walls of the house the world
impends, steadily pressing, we have our guns they whisper
we have our armies, dear, we brought them for you, smell
taste

my police forces, my careless cocktails of whose words
will and whose will not, whose voice will and whose will
not, whose blood will and whose will not, whose girl are
you?

come ride with me in my wonderful machina. i have eaten
bigger trees than you and nourished larger pockets than
you will ever be. sleep with me and i can make all of this
o

putting our lives on the line to make a better world here
now turning my womb inside out to show here how now
this exposé o release me dammit, if i can just rest i can
think

beyond the machinery of state that has got us patiently
waiting for more of the same to the good, or more of the
same to the treacherous side of creation. breathe slow and
deep

bodily boldly okay. i can make a girl a man a poem a home
i can taste wind and the sea flowing over all of the impending
to tell me and by virtue of telling me telling you but just
listen

draw on the well like i told you, here, all you have learned
of the world you can use to make a new one a green and a
blue one with all the autumn colours and the deep surprising
nature

of the flowers. you can make the excellent sea the restful
day you can make or house a point and for the pleasure of
the ancestors and in the vindication of all of the lost i have
found

i will do this, just and joyous, but for now try to sleep and if
i can make a make or a life i will if i can i will i told you, here
draw listen sing soon wait wait wait o darling, despite the fire
arms

leaning up against the walls of the house know the just men are
after all just men, and can be persuaded and yet may succumb.
i will keep synthesizing danger and truth and making beauty for
you

while others will carry our names, and do the same for me too.
we are a safe well of creation and the well of danger no deeper
than us. the ancestors, the new words, the poets, the old words
the wrong roads

and the right relationships unfurling on a cloudy day. and i know
the sun's light. i know the clarity. i can find my words and the will
to finish what was started and to strengthen what was weakened that
day.

In English, "south of the walls of the north / *a poem for Angye Gaona & for her daughter*," in Spanish, "Para Angye Gaona y su hija" (translated by Susana Wald).

A Colombian poet, active in international poetry circles and mother of a young girlchild, finds herself under house arrest. Her international friends, mainly surrealist poets, undertake a collective pushback in hopes of avoiding (and not aggravating or complicating) judicial excess. Reading Angye's work in translation, viewing playful photographs of herself and her daughter, and responding out of my own deep well of experience of mothering the small in sometimes extremely conscribed circumstance, the poem emerges with uncharacteristic long lines and a wall-like form.

In discussing the world of literature, or the news, there are the distinctions (countries of Europe, Canada's friends) and the indistinctions (South America, Africa, Asia). The English title responds directly to this imbalance of knowledge and information, and to the gates across U.S. and Israel which reflect we have learned no good thing since the fall of the Berlin wall. An attempt to wall away the wealthy countries from those that are for extraction only, to keep the human rights on one side and the imbalances firmly in place.

Likewise, the walls are those of language, and collective associations. Access to literary and current events is brokered and filtered by the smaller group, of every community, who can and will create a passage of art or fact through the extraordinary ordinary powers of translation.

Giving voice to dangerous intimacies, and illuminating the place of the Madonna / the woman / the mother in the web of the world, is the work of the poem. Narrative leaps about, swift shifts in direction to address the oceanic general trends and the small specifics. Ultimately it is hopeful, an affirmation.

ten anonymous journeys

coal clouds and gulls hang steady in the wind
songs, scuffles, shuffles, screams, receipts
paper ways of mean

dream arteries surge seaward
pistons beat, engines screech
and a cacophonous wind thunders

barnacled black hulls slice and sluice out
through the streaming scheldt from antwerp

the port delivers the coal and cargo
erosions ripple over memory
slip the border
lost in the rip
of tide

they feed the loss
my body brims and bleeds into the thick air against the atlantic

sisters, brothers, cousins, and great ancestors pass in quiet

———————   masters schmidt and theiles,
eye the violence in the waters
the flap clap wind shifts
a pattern
the deep distance, the long droning notes of my lungs

———————   we curl into the confluence of the labrador
breaking through contrarian waves

my hulled hands crash against the tide   ———————

to the unloved I will offer

a part of me

in hope my wards will be made complete

for another life   ———————

while my indentured life escapes me

admire me then
    do so when
this beauty subsides
      when my name ages
        do so when i transmute, shift my name
          and become the ss *komagata maru*

—∿—

In an earlier version of "ten anonymous journeys," I included a link to the Library and Archives Canada site where one can view the ten citations and passenger lists for the ship that brought thousands of European immigrants to the new world (Canada and the U.S.).[1] Before it was named the SS *Komagata Maru*, this newly built ship (circa 1890) was known at that time as the SS *Stubbenhuk* and SS *Sicilia*. The ship was owned first by the Hansa Line and then the Hamburg America Line. It was a common fixture along the trade and migration routes between Hamburg, Italy, Greece and New York, Montreal and Quebec City.

The front section of *dream / arteries* is entitled "soul-journ to the end of the pacific." Like the other poems in this sequence, I utilized the following format: a historical quote, archival citation or pseudo entry, followed by a poem. Overall this approach was taken except in a few circumstances where I decided the quote took away from the verse, which was the case with this poem.

One discourse-related piece I will add is my exploration of Mikhail Bakhtin's notion of "chronotope" in literary text analysis. There were two reasons I explored this further in *dream / arteries*: one was to constrict time and create a fluid dream time-space that would assemble fragmented note items within the poem, biographical identification (sea captains) and bring life to the poem through the movement on the Atlantic. What is not stated but alluded to are two distinct systems for migration documentation: one is as public record and the other is as surveillance record; as is the case of the photographs of the Punjabi passengers of the Komagata Maru.

The second reason was to create a reverse-time presence to the subject matter of the poem. By embedding a translucent peripheral or marginal brief optic stamp placed behind the text, I hope the reader gains a level of ambiguity to how the ship and its documented history are perceived in that moment. In coupling the poems with the ghosted out image of the *Komagata Maru* passengers, there is a further blurring of time, histories and the global movement of people, and collectively they add to a lingering sadness the ship images bring, even though the photos are taken 20 years into the future.

Overall I am hoping that while this poem reads fluidly across a space-time-dream-time structure, some specific questions arise for the reader, as they did for me during the research and writing of the poems.

[1] Library and Archives Canada, Immigration Records, Passenger Lists 1865-1922—Stubbenhuk.

WAYDE COMPTON

WHITHER HOGAN'S ALLEY?

Examination of Blighted District Undertaken by Civic Body

BY DICKENSON FOYLE

Hogan's Alley, the block-long unpaved lane running from Station Street to Gore Avenue between Union and Prior streets, is known to residents of Vancouver's East End for its squalid mixture of decrepit shacks, run-down tenements, and—like echoes of a former, more pastoral time—the odd cottage or stable.

Ask the average Vancouverite what comes to mind when you mention Hogan's Alley and he will immediately offer up tales of crime, immorality and destitution (stories heard second or third-hand, he will quickly assure you). However, is Hogan's Alley truly a "mark of Cain" upon our city's otherwise un-blemished complexion, as many would claim, or is it merely a convenient scapegoat for the sins of the entire metropole?

For city officials, it now appears, this question is less important than the one unavoidable reality: Hogan's Alley is a slum. Thus, to-day, members of the city's departments of building and sanitation paid a visit to the neighbour-hood in order to appraise for them-selves the true extent of its dissipation.

For the law, however, there is no question that this concentration of ramshackle buildings and tawdry hotels contribute to and exemplify the larger district's criminal caste, with a reach stretching out for blocks in all directions.

Asked for his impression of Ho-gan's Alley, Constable Mark Macfie of-fers without hesitation, "It's bootleggers and gamblers and prostitutes from one end to the other. All manner of profes-sional layabouts and unsavoury types dwell there." Pressed to account for the neighbourhood's lowly state, Constable Macfie draws our regard to endemic overcrowding: "They keep themselves packed-in tight down there, like cords of sisal. It's like a hive. And the bootleg-gers and pickpockets and every-man-jack of those morphine peddlers are the queen bees."

Long-time resident Hadrian McCabe, a Negro and retired foundry worker, weighs the question of the dis-trict's crisis diplomatically: "This place has its church people and its good-time people just like everywhere else. Some of these buildings are raggedy, but most of them are clean and doing just fine." Asked if the city officials should take the neighbourhood in hand by pulling down the seediest shacks and cleaning up the crime, the Ameri-can-born McCabe remarks, "I suppose you can take away the ones that are collapsing down, but mostly it's just fine." When asked about the rampant crime for which his neighbourhood is notorious, he only shrugs, saying, "Those aren't the troubles people down here talk about most often."

Nevertheless, the final say about this controversial area may well belong to city officials presently at work in-specting its every dimension. Though the civic committee, composed of building department engineers, health inspectors, and city sanitation officials under the direction of council-appoint-ed social services director Cecil Grey, has no direct power to enact policy, its probe will undoubtedly prove influen-tial in future strategies for concretizing the neighbourhood's salvation.

—∾—

Though it looks like journalism, "Whither Hogan's Alley?" is part of a long poem cycle called "Rune." The larger poem discusses how the city of Vancouver gutted its own East End during a mid-20th century "urban renewal" scheme, one that ultimately sacrificed the black community, once centralized at Hogan's Alley, and levelled it for the creation of a viaduct. The hegemonic thinking behind such treatment can be tracked in newspaper articles such as the one my poem satirizes, a story by a journalist named Jack Stepler called "Hogan's Alley Fate At Stake" printed in Vancouver's *Daily Province* in 1939.

I'm interested in and curious about the language of injustice, the rhetorical pre-emptive strikes so often used by power to rationalize repression. So I wanted to "translate" Stepler's original article, with all its condescension and disgust for the poor, to explore its ideology. (His summary of a whole community of people is, for example: "To the average citizen, Hogan's Alley stands for three things—squalor, immorality and crime.") I rewrote Stepler in order to inhabit him, to wear his language and walk around in it, to see for a moment from the vantage of his hostility, to scry his spite for some kind of sense.

The ghost who showed up when I wrote was the character Hadrian McCabe. (His name is a wall built against barbarians; he works at a *foundry*, the referent of the word *ghetto*.) The author-character-mask, Foyle, who is McCabe's discursive foil, interviews him, but they speak past each other, utterly askew. Foyle distances McCabe as "American-born" like it negates the man's presence; and he asks the leading questions that the city seems to require as it sets in motion the eventual destruction of the place.

What Stepler would never have heard, I hear, while inhabiting the hide of his language. The failure and rupture of this poetic experiment is in one of McCabe's sentences that emerged, the one where the real meaning languishes, not out of reach, but unreached for: "Those aren't the troubles people down here talk about most often." The failure of urban renewal was in the trouble never asked after.

vanishing point

> *Pedestrian motor functions ... create one of those "true systems whose existence actually makes the city."*
> – Michel de Certeau

map making
exclusive use
newspaper box
penthouse suite
huddling for warmth
tactile
uniform

> *spatial practices in fact secretly structure the determining conditions of social life*

definition
anomaly
institution
pre-eminent
dilated pupils crack cataract
panoptician
gentle
kingly
familiar

and the underpass was the only cover

aberration
walk it off
deal
deal with it
deal with it until tomorrow
no phoenix and gutbusted
all the plans fell apart

even emily won't talk to me anymore, my own goddamn sister

fumigate
contradiction
political technology

coffee the only saviour
differentiate
city's common practitioners dwell
hallmarked for destruction
understanding eludes us
geographic
coat and boot comprehension
hair slicked back with grease
temporary arrangement
leprous apparently

> *urban life allows what has been excluded from it by*
> *the urbanistic plan to increase even further*

tracks and paths
trains and veins
melodrama
gridded
influx
cunning and stubborn
management network
derail
epic struggled
systems analyst
space maker
rationalization
ground level
old converse behind the fire escape
discipline
bread
controlled operations
uncontrolled utterances

> *The relics of meaning, and sometimes their shells, the inverted*
> *leftovers of great ambitions, maybe for walking*

outside the sphere
invisible
fragmentation

bracketed
clean space
transgression
structure of a myth
stylish interiors
red blanket
coded tranmission
four-inch blade
gaps, slips and allusions
symbolism
furniture
encounter

What / where is the "vanishing point"—of people? Of the city? Who decides the boundaries and the zones of living / permanence? What is the role of the interstitial in this process? How does the "citizen" fit into the urban in ways that the "denizen" is excluded? These are questions I was "poetically" stalking, especially as I moved about the city myself.

Systems of control / analysis / direction are confounded, reworked, dismantled, and eventually circumvented in the forms of life and living that elude these processes—the life of the pedestrian, the "spatial practice" of movement in and around the urban space.

Structures of meaning that are erected / designed via spheres of control attempt to impose the "city from above," but the flux and flow of life in the urban space does not meet this process evenly, if at all. Which is to say, in the end, that the city is *conceived* from above but *lived* from below. Gaps are a part of both the design and implementation of systems of control, but the pedestrian, the city dweller, are constantly renegotiating, bypassing and altogether eradicating these boundaries. The gap becomes the antithesis of system. The underpass is cleared of weeds and obstacles by the pedestrian. The "derelict" enclosure is fenced in, cut open and reworked, becomes park, becomes domestic.

The interstitial is more than the alley, the narrow cut between buildings; it is the zone of existence in both the physical and social sense for many. I fixed on de Certeau's ideas here because they embrace the vision of the urban space as recreated / torqued / redefined by the "spatial practice" of the pedestrian. To me, this both acknowledges and creates possibility for hope for those who elude the normative systems of the urban space and its design—the "kingly / familiar" for whom "the underpass was the only cover." Exclusion, revision, and the interstitial become a cuneiform of writing the city.

ELIZABETH BACHINSKY

Hearsay in the Valley of Condominiums

I am writing to tell you: that story
I'd overhead about those pygmy

remains? It ran as a practical joke on
the part of city planners or some

local newspaper flunky; I'm not
sure which. Bridge construction went

ahead as planned.
There were, and are, no pygmies on that land.

And, furthermore, that kids' water
park town council tore

down to replace with a yuppie gas station,
is not a gas station.

It is an improved playground.
I got confused when they tore the old

stuff out. For a while, it looked like they
were building a gas station. They

weren't. This "new" water park is, apparently,
more environmentally sound. Which is not to say

that yuppies aren't moving into the area
in droves, because they are.

And the new mayor,
who is also a gangster,

plans to turn his offices into
a Starship Bingo.

I wrote "Hearsay in the Valley of Condominiums" when I was living in Maple Ridge Park in 2004. I'd just finished my Masters Degree at UBC and I'd moved back to my hometown to be writer-in-residence at the Maple Ridge Arts Centre. The local Arts Council had put me up in a house in the middle of the park and every day on my way into town I'd drive past the children's water park on the corner of 232nd Street and Fern Crescent. One day I drove past and there was a blue plastic fence up around the water park. There were signs attached to the fence that said SUPER SAVE. SUPER SAVE is the name of a chain of gas stations. It is also the name of a rental company that rents fences. I was familiar with the chain of gas stations. I'd never heard of the rental company. For weeks I drove past that fence thinking, *What a bunch of assholes. Building a gas station over top of the water park.* Soon enough, I'd tell anyone I met about the gas station going up over the water park. And where would the kids cool off in the summer? And did we really need more gas stations? And isn't Maple Ridge Park a provincial park? And so on.

The thing about rumours is that there is always a little truth in them. Just enough to make whatever story you're spinning plausible. That's what makes them thrive. The fence company is the same company that owns the chain of grocery stores. The mayor really did want to build a casino in the heart of town (eventually he did!). Bridge construction was happening. Condos were going up. Maple Ridge was changing. But gas stations? Pygmies? Not so much. Gangsters? Dear reader, I'll let you decide.

Eventually, my husband corrected me. *No no no, he said. The city is upgrading the water park. That's a fence to keep kids out while they're doing the renovation.* So then I had to take back every mean thing I'd said about the Park Board and the municipal government. Only there was no way to know exactly how many people to whom I'd spread my moronic rumour. I thought, oh this is exactly how rumours get started and I wrote my poem.

DENNIS E. BOLEN

Everybody

Everybody knew somebody

    Age of battered pickup
    cigarette load ashtray butt

Everybody knew

    grease coif armpit stain
    snagglepick match tooth

    Beyond
only the responsibly parented survive...

Everybody knew beltless toddler

Everybody

    Unrestrain seat bench projectile
    to the outskirts of wisdom

    Everybody knew somebody dead
    of car wreck

        Undershirt men
        cross-eye sway fatigue
        pace toward a next shift
        to hew and draw and maintain
    skirted metal house with wheels
    rented concrete

    Smoke death and like it

everybody knew

    to cull those lucky not otherwise demised
    of proud ignorance

Everybody knew

    none should crave education
    Drop out by 16 or you're not a man

Everybody knew

    alcoholic
    frown drink burp asleep
    door-slam solitary

Everybody knew men curse pregnant women

Weep
Shout
Things broken

        When the truck flies everybody off the road
        swat the kid who won't shut up
        fiddle the dial radio
        Leaden sad song
        soon silence

—∞—

Everybody: *"The First Place on a Road Map to This Poet's Current Emotional Location."*

My arrival to poetry from long decades of fiction and arts journalism occurred as a solution to the problem presented by the volume of memory I had and the time it would take to transform all that data into the kind of written entertainment I prefer to convey upon the world. "Everybody" popped up amid initial attempts to jot down childhood impressions—not just memory, but feelings—about the era of time I was living in. As anyone can sense by the reading, as a child I was not exactly thrilled about my environment or those populating it around me at the time.

In fact I chose this poem to open my collection of similarly acidic, atmospherically lugubrious "industrial poems" because it serves more or less as a précis to much that follows (*cigarette... armpit... rented concrete... proud ignorance*) and encapsulates a distaste and at least some of my dismay at the world I found myself in. The piece is meant to instill a notion of detachment to the scene(s) illustrated, a not-so-objective assessment of the situation, and a permanent disdain for stasis... a yearning to get out.

The rest of the book—*Black Liquor*—could be considered a journal of that departure commitment, a running notebook of constant movement toward somewhere undefined but definitely not the land of *"Weep / Shout / Things broken."* Thus, "Everybody" could well be subtitled "Everything," but it certainly serves my purposes—particularly in the "travel" imagery of the final stanza—in linking the semi-rural world with the uber-urban scenarios employed in later stages of the collection.

Flesh Pot

Born, muscle bound,
Backboned, map, matrix-
Mother intact
Into families, slums

Manors, private
Security firms, institutions.
Pirates or the pious
We flourish. Raw teeth, germs,

Clubfeet do not impede us,
Rank and garbled speech fleeting
As tin Jeeps. Our struggle
Barbie-doll drama, tumult banal,

Pain prosaic, strife fuelling ripeness,
Gauntlets passed through swiftly
Until the day we drop. Nominated,
Cornered, required to wither

Under the gun,
Succumb, for we remain
That tender, precious human
Flesh terminators aim for.

—∿—

The news. As dismaying as the news may be, it infiltrates. I am no longer surprised that nothing changes, progresses, the word *progress* is quaint. With all the information we digest daily, we know we are not moving forward, that we are merely swept up. To preserve a stance of one's own is heroic, a valiant albeit futile effort, for the individual cannot withstand an avalanche of humanity. The life force. Our flesh, our pitiful armour, is as ephemeral as our lives. We are equally invincible and weak, eternal and temporal, resilient and susceptible, susceptible to the machinations of machines, technology. Human nature is a constant, though we are as tough and logical as salmon swimming upstream, as evolved as a grizzly bear. We are driven, brilliant, vainglorious and misguided as Frankenstein. I might have titled it "Natural Order." That's all the poem speaks to. Portrays. The flesh came first, flesh responsible for the monster.

ROB TAYLOR

The Wailing Machines

I wanted to say: look, this intersection, this place
where we have come together and stopped traffic,
is the only place we ever could have met, you and I—
pistons that never before aligned, even when the engine
was at rest, that had to wait until the whole contraption
burst and we were spilled out onto the pavement to see that yes,
all those hints—those darting noises, glints of steam and light—
held truth, that there are others as startled and ragged as ourselves,
and somehow gaining that knowledge seems worth all this blood
and bother and traffic lined up over the crest of the hill.
I wanted to say all of this, but my throat sputtered
which is why I merely waved as we were lifted away
and placed inside the wailing machines
we were only beginning to know to imagine.

I wrote "The Wailing Machines" after viewing the aftermath of a car accident at the intersection of First Avenue and Commercial Drive—the cars were still a mess, the ambulances were just pulling away, and the crowd that had formed was slowly dispersing. I had been living on Commercial Drive for two years at the time, and it was the third such accident I'd come upon. This makes sense in that First Avenue is the only major street which crosses through the middle of the cultural and social heart of Commercial Drive: a meeting place of two very different paces of life and sets of preoccupations.

As a child of Vancouver's suburbs, and a resident of Commercial Drive, I felt a connection with each—here was, here is, one of the few places where disparate parts of our city intersect, and the only times we really stop to look at one another are in these moments of failure and violence.

In its way, I like to think of "The Wailing Machines" as an encouragement to see each other more, and more generously, in the moments between disasters. To notice and validate one another's existence. To rescue each other from our well-constructed and well-policed invisibilities.

CHRISTINE LECLERC

1.

We listen to water.
We go float in it.

The ocean makes us giggle.
    We giggle when we're in it.

But no matter how advocacy voice demands our sketches, the future is far from shapeless. The future is already flush with months, minutes and—

hear something

—

assholes. It has power, movements and press releases. And it's full of soundtracks to make you feel you've just seen a movie, like your life is something—

hard to leave

—like a supertanker.

Interim service begins on Midcontinent Express Pipeline.

Kinder Morgan announces open season for crude oil shipments
        on Cochin pipeline

Louisiana pipeline in service.
Rockies Express pipeline begins service on Rex-East.
Kinder Morgan completes first commercial shipment of
        biodiesel in U.S.—

            linger

                        —on
                        Plan-
                        tation
                        pipe
                        -line.

In 2012, I worked on a banner hang. The banner was massive in size and the amount of time it was taking to deploy. The group brainstormed in case the banner didn't work out. One idea was to put a giant *Oilywood* sign up on the North Shore mountains. Soon after the brainstorm, the banner was unfurled over choppy water in the shipping channel that runs under Lions Gate bridge. Tar sands product is shipped here.

For me, *Oilywood* evokes urged fetishization of tar sands infrastructure. I liked the idea and explored the possibility of an installation, but consultation with First Nations and a bit of math showed me that an easier to situate and more affordable approach was needed.

Getting to know Burrard Inlet and spurring conversation about its future in the context of climate change were the main appeals of the project for me. So, I undertook a research program of audio recording water, interviewing beach goers and creating poets' maps with community members at free workshops.

A community-based poem emerged. In *Oilywood*, language and ideas shared by people encountered around the Inlet sit in tension with Kinder Morgan's corporate messaging. The poem challenges collaborators to imagine futures that protect coast and climate.

FRED WAH

Between You and Me There is an I

Between two stools
The hyphen lies
The eggs and the nest
The blind and the fold
The hinge of the city
The door and the jamb
The map and its edges
The wars I've not fought
The life and its lease
The rope but which end
The brink and disaster
The bank and the laughter
The spike below Chinaman's Peak
That spot where the two rails meet

From between two stools
Hear the silence rise
The smoke 'round your neck
The tongue and the dash
The cat and the cradle
The dog dead in the creek
The slash and the burn
The shadows of NAFTA
The head and the tax
Rock bluff and river
The laundry its mark
The height and the trestle
Cata and strophe
Not caboose but what's after

"Between You and Me There is an I" is part of a series, "Discount Me In" which was generated out of a 2007 symposium on poetics, "Count Me In: Writing Public Selves." Its undercurrent is an attention to how the pronoun operates as a negotiable trope in a racialized discourse, specifically the site of "betweenness" with its desire to find some way to disperse the dominance of polarity around the hyphen. This attention to equivocation is perhaps a dialectic that is constitutive and generative in its recognition of a kind of "ambiguity of agency" (Judith Butler) confronted within the creative and the critical, the social and the political. Most of the conjunctive phrasings are simply repetitions, particularly from my collection *Faking It: The Poetics of Hybridity*, of my own ongoing search for a language that can help articulate and generate a more incisive public language around hybridity. I was given a piece of useful advice once by Clark Blaise, a prose fiction writer, that writing is always seeking its beginning. In other words, we begin again and again. The "between two stools" phrase I picked up in *A Menorah for Athena: Charles Reznikoff and the Jewish Dilemmas of Objectivist Poetry* by Stephen Fredman. As well, both Michael Davidson's essay, "The Dream of a Public Language: Modernity, Manifesto, and the Citizen Subject," and Jeff Derksen's introduction to a recent issue of *West Coast Line*, No. 51, "Poetry and the Long Neo-liberal Moment," inform this series of poems, including this one. These poems attempt to illuminate the hyphen as a site of intervention, the gap as a space in which to generate the news and contest the manipulation of power and information by the state.

MEREDITH QUARTERMAIN

First Night

bus to Point Grey the earl I type bust
through Chinatown it's free tonight along Pender Street
wheel chair gets on bus driver kicking the seats up
with his boot strapping the chair in chair-woman
accompanied by young man & folded scooter
young woman a man's overcoat over her
shoulders they get off on Burrard Street
at the Ports store and the Royal Centre
the Vancouver Hotel all aglitter—we
carry on past St Paul's Hospital its star-shaped
strings its rainbow arches of lights Davie Street
a block later squeegee kid on his haunches
on a rim of asphalt at a gas station squeegee
and plastic pop bottle of water in the shadows
of a battered hedge he pulls his feet in closer his arms
fold tighter into the folded legs his hands make
fists on the tops of his knees and he bows his head
into the fists a small scrunched skeleton
in thin hood as though to sleep against the buses
and cars roaring past too fast to run out and clean
windshields for a loonie

on the way back in the first hour of the first
day a crowd on Point Grey smoking pot
hey there's the bus run for it Happy
New Year Happy New Year the bus
jammed with jolly people tiny pointed
hats rainbow coloured wands
a woman with pink hair another
with earrings flashing lights blue and red
all starry-eyed crowds at Burrard's Bridge
the San Fiorenzo 42 guns no room no room
lights on the bows and wheelhouses of boats
at the wharves
Premier Smithe's attorney Davie street
someone in a blanket under a shop awning
no room no room till the Royal Centre

strangers hugging in the street youths high-
fiving it whooping yelling at the bus wheel-chair
woman the same one cannot get on no way
to know she cd've if she'd wheeled to the next
stop turn right on Pender past Malone's Pub
the Vancouver Vocational Institute
Tinseltown mall the Chinatown gate Asian man
working woman off shift get on ragged
haggard streetmen no parties
for them shops dark buildings of brick not
plate glass turn the corner at Gore the concrete
viaduct the warehouses for produce the small
dusty homes cheek by jowl on Prior
Edward Gawler shareholder Vancouver Improvement
Company chainlink fences around matchbox yards
I type years patched in porches and bare
lightbulbs clashing siding rickety steps
the poorer older the first Vancouver
that has not the means of Tiffany lamps grand
pianos wide porches stone pillars
has not the means of
gardens and views
happy new year
it's free tonight

Written around 2001, the poem records a bus trip through downtown Vancouver on New Year's Eve and the return trip in the early hours of the new year. I travelled from my house in Strathcona to spend the evening with Robin Blaser in Point Grey, a much wealthier part of town. The bus went along Prior Street, Pender Street, Burrard Street, over Burrard Bridge and along Cornwall Avenue and returned on the same route.

The great poets of place, such as Charles Olson writing on Gloucester, William Carlos Williams writing on Paterson, and especially Daphne Marlatt writing on Steveston, were all present to me when I wrote this poem and others in *Vancouver Walking*. When I started writing about Vancouver, I wanted a way to break through the surface of normalness in city streets, some way to disrupt the unquestioned presence of colonial skyscrapers on aboriginal land. History became the way to do that. Whose names were on the streets? Hence the reference to Burrard and his ship the *San Fiorenzo*, and Premier Smithe and Alexander Davie, men who got into government for business connections and land grabs, not social welfare, and Edward Gawler Prior, part of a prominent real estate company. Why are their names on streets and not the First People's? Why no women's names?

Landscapes, cityscapes, are not just givens, not abstract "objective" reality that's simply there. Rather we make up landscapes as we go through them. I wanted to change the lens from fantasy objectivity to a multi-dimensional city through time, the city as a crossroads of a personally felt world and the historical factors that shaped it, a crossroads of histories from all sorts of stakeholders. I wanted to take account of the ground where I was standing, the physical ground, the historical ground, the cultural ground, and the linguistic ground.

Save the receipts

No word in corporate
News of fire
The road insists
Road closures
The sidewalk fits
Our detour

Filmed arrests
Paraphernalia
Motivated violence
Fixtures hauled away
just a couple of days
1-888-JUSTICE

Weekly threat
Assessments
Time sheets
Pick pocket wallet
Weighted
Four or five figure bills

Easer to haver
Dispersal dregs
Partial proceeds
Shipped to the sticks
Tricking back lanes
Comments are closed

Social safe guard
Tents in parks
Threshold of appalling
Blues as distance
Service disturbing
Suck City

Commercial vistas
Look laws
Affect statistics
Workers overhead shout
Cheap appliances
Get your ATM here

Blues as distance. On a clear day down the Main Street corridor to CRAB Park in Vancouver the atmosphere softens the view to the North Shore's receding ridgelines; the aerial perspective harkening blues that lift me. After a meal in Wendy Poole Park I used to round out my half-hour lunch with a walk to the lion statues on the bridge, to offer a silent lament to the Two Sisters.

This poem touches on the everyday crises of homelessness, "development," construction, noise, and indifference in a neighbourhood, the Downtown Eastside, beset by systemic and direct violence. I wrote this in proximity to the Safe Streets Act preceding the Olympics that fuelled aggressive policing, "street sweeps," no-gos, and intimidation that led to the removal of many low-income, often racialized and Indigenous residents and ushered in new consumers. That old story. This is where I work and volunteer most of my days. The poem intersects with daily administrative tasks, payroll and petty cash, as I am unable to extract myself from the narrative.

I hear Tom Waits' "Falling Down", "it's a lot smaller down here on the ground" and document how "Suck City" turns away (as the "elms grow sparse / black-spotted parasols"). In the neighbourhood we notice an increase in designer dogs toward the Gastown perimeter. The missing posters of women that have dotted the city for decades elicit less empathy than that one say, for the bichon frise (there's an award!) missing since Sunday. In the line "easer to haver" I conflate street artist Easer's tag with the lyric "I know it's easy to have me" from the Okkervil River song *Red*, heartbreakingly aware of trauma and of mothers' and daughters' estrangement. "Save the receipts" is a column of poetry grown frail under the weight of NGO-facilitated justice, strengthened by word of sacred fires lit.

SONNET L'ABBÉ

XXXIII

Free music lulls many angry, tailored-suited youth. Some mornings, the avenues bristle when *flâneurs* mutter under their custom foulards; the fountains stop: swish-clothed street lovers keep plugging into audile cyberspace, blocking the polis' chorusing whirl. The gay, bold, mean-faced theatrics of meanderers and widowers grants gentlemen gilded standing; on pedestals they stand, dreaming address with heavenly adolescents. Their myspace nostalgia can permutate into Spotify fetishes if bass pleasures are met. Soundclouds float above transit riders' worn outfits; thugly rackets wonh-wonh in streetcars' packed aisles. Palatial factories are renoed; lofty rooms with retrofits, tongue-and-groove floors, and walk-in closets draw lads; rough industrial visages hide sensitively aligned designer sound systems. Bearded downtown aesthetes wink at hot hipster ladies, Instagram charitable events, omg at boys in uniform, learn lines by black rap lyric masters to earn cred with kids. Their shiny bikes with brass bells, their Triumphs, make noisy streetscapes. Listeners endeavour to earn money by growing handlebar mustaches for full-time jobs at blacksmithesque wear-houses, but only scarce hourly minimum wages do they score. Plugged into online clouds, while apathy masks hide their misfortunes, some men discover Wild Style. Those hip hop mofos were the hippest, mixing vinyl on vintage turntables, in ghettos whitefolk disdained. The suburban sons of bitches who overlord municipal folky festivals entertain wishes involving heavy metal frontmen, substances, and gun-straddling angels of death.

—⚬—

This poem is the thirty-third in what will be a series of 154 poems: the project is called *Sonnet's Shakespeare: 154 Ecolonizations*. In this series I take each of Shakespeare's sonnets and "write over" them. This is my play with the mode of erasure poetry, one that hides the original text in plain sight, and attempts a muted bivocality in the reading experience.

For example, the first words of Shakespeare's "Sonnet 33" are:

Full many a glorious morning have I seen

The first line of my colonized sonnet, "XXXIII," is as follows:

Free music lulls many angry, tailored-suited youth.
Some mornings, the avenues bristle when

I envision my process as analogous to colonialization, to riding roughshod over the "traditional territory" of English literature and imposing upon it my own descriptions of the world. My poems restage the colonizer's capacity not only to erase but to reframe the stories of colonized people, to "talk over" existing voices so loudly that the cultures are, at important levels of voice, silenced. Though colonizers often nearly destroy the legibility of original cultures, they are never fully successful at erasing the original cultures they mean to displace.

In this poem, I think the first word that came to me from looking at the word "full" was "lull," and I started asking myself about things that anesthetize, that lull, and then the "u" and the "m" must have suggested music. "Free music." I thought I would be off on a tear about intellectual property, but then those angry, dapper youth showed up, and those avenues, and soon I found myself in the imaginative territory of a morning commute on public transit, a movement propelled by economies, during which some of us soothe and insulate ourselves via the aesthetic order of our curated playlists. As I worked, the poem emerged as a comment on the classes of people that share (or don't share) Canadian urban spaces and soundscapes with one another.

I'm very aware that no aboriginal or "Indian" language made it into this poem. The presence of "the Indian" is very important to me in this project, and that presence informs a majority of the poems in this series. I may yet fix the absence in this one.

CALVIN WHARTON

Tracey Calls

I just got another call from TRACEY who called because she was asked by SEARS to call people out of the blue (which happens to be the colour of the shirt I'm wearing today), and find out what sorts of thoughts they might have about SEARS stores. She sounded like a nice person, so I wasn't rude to her and I didn't threaten to call the police to get her to stop harassing me. Instead, I told her I'd think about SEARS as much as possible in the next few days and I'd get back to her.

Yes, I was lying, but I don't think I'll burn in HELL for a little white lie.

I mentioned it was "another call" because someone called me on Friday and I'm pretty sure that was TRACEY, too. But I told her then I was much too busy with IMPORTANT MATTERS to spend any time discussing a department store with her. Another lie (about the important matters). I guess it's true what they say: tell a lie and they start piling up all over the place.

I feel sorry for TRACEY and all her telephone-soliciting brethren and sistren. It's not her fault that SEARS wants to know my thoughts about their stores, and will pay her GOOD MONEY to find out.

I think that what she does is a little bit like FISHING, only a darker, weirder, more intrusive kind of fishing than I've ever done.

The source of the poem is obvious, I suppose: the ubiquitous, of-our-age, junk phone call. At best, the voices of the anonymous call-centre workers are like cathedral bells, the calling of their *calling* reminding us of when and where and who we are. At best.

One morning I answered the phone to be greeted by a woman who identified herself as Tracey. My wife and I had bought a mattress from Sears, and Tracey's task was to gauge our customer satisfaction via some questions that would only take a few minutes of our time. And though I sympathized with her having to do this kind of work—this dark fishing—I felt we had already done enough by purchasing the mattress, so said I was busy.

The prose poem variation generally doesn't occur to me, or perhaps doesn't often feel comfortable. In this case, the nature of the narrative impetus for the poem allowed, or encouraged, this approach. Content suggesting form.

The words in all caps are intended to provide points of emphasis, and to help transform the prose into a poem. One attempt to subvert the demands of the narrative. And, if successful, they also establish a bit of distraction to facilitate the double turn (at the end of stanza three, and again in the final lines).

About lies: Some elements of this poem have been fabricated, some have been altered, some are as they happened. I tell my students that poetry is not reportage. There is another, more important standard of authenticity and accuracy the poet aims for. With luck, a poem will find its way to the genuine and even, sometimes, to the true.

The End of the War

The year you were born women killed their children
when they learned their husbands were dead
then gave themselves up to the same dark eye; the war
finally over, confetti in the streets, Mussolini strung up
in Piazza Loreto, Hitler dead in Berlin.
ss soldiers blowing themselves up to avoid surrender.
Everywhere broken skin on fists, collapsed buildings,
the abstract of bodies that are no longer
bodies, that become the grey webbing of dreams.

In those days there wasn't anything humans couldn't do—
raze a city, stall time, kill what it was we once gave life to.
The stopped clock in the city square told us nothing,
the house that stood on the edge of obliteration swayed once,
then gave in. The wind that crossed the continent circled the globe
carrying death's ashes, then came back to us again.

Still, in the slack of all that dying, in the fierce distension
of birth, something endured. You saw the world differently.
For you it hung like a sturdy door. This room leading to
        that room
and on to the next. The sound of your cry coming back
with a soft answer. The distance between you and pure possibility,
as navigable as a finger running over a map. And the future?
The span of time that follows night. The brightness of those
first few hours of morning.

—⟨⟨⟨—

"The End of the War" had three major influences. The first was a photograph taken by Margaret Bourke-White in 1945 (reproduced in the photograph collection *Century*) of a German mother who had murdered her children (who were laid out on a rug in the photo) and who would then go on to kill herself after her "Nazi" husband had died and the war had ended.

The second influence was the man the poem is dedicated to—my friend Martin Levin who is the "you" of the poem. I think the poem was written after I'd met his wonderful parents at their home in Winnipeg because the last few lines of the poem have always evoked (for me) images of their house and the family photographs they kept on the wall—photographs that presenced the dead members of their family at mealtimes. Maybe it's for that reason that I always read "morning" (the poem's last word) as a homonym for mourning—the two different outcomes of a war: living to see another day because one has survived, or death and the fallout that is grief: a mourning that was only possible when the war had ended.

The third influence, palpable in the poem I think, is the destruction of lived spaces—of urban centres, monumental architecture, of homes. *Century* is full of photographs of razed cities (from London to Stalingrad) and the photograph of the mother standing over the children she killed is that of an interior of a nice urban or suburban home: wood furniture with spindle legs, a handwoven rug, a painting. My mother was born in 1943, my friend Martin was born in 1945. I have always wondered what mark being born in the midst of such a horrible war might leave on babies—what they inherited from a destabilized and wounded world, when perhaps their own tight and closed worlds seemed so stable.

COLIN BROWNE

Go straight for two blocks, through the light, past Starbucks to the next
one, take a right at Holt Renfrew, then a left at the big white place on the
corner with insoluble teeth, left again at the checkpoint, straight ahead for
six blocks to the underpass, you'll see the Big Carrot, then right, follow the
tracks along the steel fence to the tank farm, keep going, veer left at the
intersection until you get to Tim Hortons, drive on for a hundred yards to the
old stadium, take a deke down the lane to your right, stay on track, watch for
mines, then right, up the boulevard for two k., turn left, then left again where
the field hospital was by the pound, continue to the cenotaph at the Lambo-
rghini dealership, duck down, gun it to the next intersection at Bed, Bath &
Beyond—remember K-Cup Packs?—take a left, go straight through to Third
on the flashing light, left on Sixth, skirt the furnaces and Thrifty's to the park
where they dumped the scorched books, roll up your window, take another
left and go up the hill until you see the drone blimps and the Japadog truck,
try a right if the Safety Centre's ring-road's open, if not do a u-ey, drive up
to the dead end by the big evangelical church, cross over the median and
return back down the hill in the bike lane until you get to what's left of City
Hall and turn right there, through the checkpoint with the road gangs—little
Tommy Tinker, is that you there in your breechclout?—keep moving slowly, do
not stop to talk.

—ᵐᵐ—

Conquest and dispossession are at the heart of The City; beneath the sidewalk cafés one finds the layered bones and sorrows of the vanquished. Cities change hands, and after the turmoil there is a longing for transfiguration. Yet the triumph of the new somehow becomes the fulfillment of an ancient or mythic prophecy—a shroud of enchantment to temper the discovery that the city's destiny, its commerce, its woes and its creative and intellectual glories, are the harvest of the original wound. Until it is extinguished, the city in each of its variations remains the child of its origins, subject to the violent unravelling stitched into its parturition. Its bottom nature, to use Gertrude Stein's phrase, is fixed, unalterable.

Some cities are likened to the offspring of a divine or supernatural ancestor, the die from which their genius and their hubris are cast. Vancouver and British Columbia were once referred to as "God's country." Not all the elect were blessed equally; they never are. The old empire has been superseded by a new empire. I haven't heard the phrase recently. When I began to write the poem below, I imagined a population in thrall to criminally-attained international investment capital menaced by climate change, globalization, income inequality and, eventually, a fear of imminent attack or invasion, which is to say an enclave of greed, thugocracy and parochialism obsessed with security. I imagined an urban landscape with subtle barriers to keep the many from the few. A driver might discover that familiar streets and landmarks have been quietly altered and that mandatory GPS upgrades have been redacted to conceal surveillance and security facilities. (Paper maps will be scarce and precious.) A lost traveller would have no recourse but to pull over, pluck up his or her courage, roll down the window, and ask for directions.

JEN CURRIN

The Oceans

The work has been done, now will you just be honest about it?

You're at home applying for an artist's grant

& I'm making sauerkraut with six friends.

"I feel your seaweed body bending my way."

Is that what you said?

Or was it the crying yoga teacher

talking about cancer & revolution?

She's still out biking in the sun,

hamburgers after chemo & much laughter.

When a nuclear plant is destabilized, we taste it

in every neighbourhood, hear it

ringing in our ears.

I want to hold my friends who survived

the debris of that tall city

& tell them not to worry

but even though we are all worried

as another wave looms.

"The fact is, we live in a city, & cities are busy,"

the yoga teacher explained. "I did an experiment.

One day I smiled at everyone on the bike path &

the next day I frowned."

It was after a movie about an earthquake,

what it did to seaweed & families.

To someone's wind coming across a body.

You enjoyed stimulants & taught them English for awhile

before they moved back

& started shaking. They taught you

how to look up at the luminescent trees,

how to take a leaf, tear it

& make a wish.

This poem was written not long after Fukushima. I was thinking a lot about the people in Japan and the oceans, about radiation—how radiation knows no borders. I was thinking about communities, relationships, neighbourhoods; experiments in kindness and unkindness; about the effects of radiation on bodies, plants, water. I was thinking about English as a sort of radiation, its role in pushing forward a global capitalist ideology, and how the speaker of the poem, a teacher of English, is complicit in this, yet at the same time wishes to make connections with her students that are not based on this ideology. I was thinking of how students teach teachers, a common theme in the book *School*, which this poem is taken from.

The cities are Vancouver and Tokyo, but really—all cities where people struggle to live connected lives.

Credits

Poems reprinted with permission from the publisher and/or author.

The poem by Jordan Abel is from *The Place of Scraps* (Talonbooks, 2013).

"south of the walls of the north" by Joanne Arnott is from *A Night for the Lady* (Ronsdale Press, 2013).

"Hearsay in the Valley of Condominiums" by Elizabeth Bachinsky is from *God of Missed Connections* (Nightwood Editions, 2009).

"Everybody" by Dennis E. Bolen is from *Black Liquor* (Caitlin Press, 2013).

"I Like Summer" by George Bowering is from *Teeth: Poems 2006–2011* (Mansfield Press, 2013).

"Walking Through a North American City, the Tenderman Picks Up a Rhythm" by Tim Bowling is from *Tenderman* (Nightwood Editions, 2011).

"Whither Hogan's Alley?" by Wayde Compton is from *Performance Bond* (Arsenal Pulp Press, 2004).

Excerpt of "Five North Vancouver Trees" by Peter Culley is from *Parkway: (Hammertown, Part 3)* (New Star Books, 2013).

"The Oceans" by Jen Currin is from *School* (Coach House Books, 2014).

"ten anonymous journeys" by Phinder Dulai is from *dreams / arteries* (Talonbooks, 2014) © Phinder Dulai. Photo detail from "Sikhs aboard ship, Komagata Maru," Canadian Photo Company, Vancouver Public Library Special Collection, accession number 136_col.

Excerpts from "How it is" by Mercedes Eng is from *Mercenary English* (CUE Books, 2013).

"riff what ought?" by Maxine Gadd is from *Subway Under Byzantium* (New Star Books, 2008).

"The Dreams We Take for Silence" by Heidi Greco is from *Igniting the Green Fuse: Four Canadian Women Poets* (Above & Beyond Productions, 2012).

"The End of the War" by Aislinn Hunter is from *The Possible Past* (Polestar, 2004).

The poem by Ray Hsu is from *Cold Sleep Permanent Afternoon* (Nightwood Editions, 2010). The poetic response by Ray Hsu was previously published in the Kootenay School of Writing's *W2010*.

"vanishing point" by Mariner Janes is from *The Monument Cycles* (Talonbooks, 2012).

The poem by Reg Johanson was originally published as a chapbook (Heavy Industries, 2011).

"Chai Tea Rant" by Wanda John-Kehewin is from *In The Dog House* (Talonbooks, 2012).

"Shower" by Fiona Tinwei Lam is from *Enter the Chrysanthemum* (Caitlin Press, 2009).

"Solitary" by Evelyn Lau is from *Living Under Plastic* (Oolichan Books, 2010).

Excerpt by Christine Leclerc is from *Oilywood* (Nomados, 2013).

"Woman Dining Alone" by Susan McCaslin is from *Light Housekeeping* (Ekstasis Editions, 1997). The poem first appeared in *The Wise Woman* (1994).

The poem by Donato Mancini is from *Fact 'N' Value* (Fillip Editions, 2011).

"through cloud" by Daphne Marlatt is from *Liquidities: Vancouver Poems Then and Now* (Talonbooks, 2013).

The excerpt from "Bird" by Kim Minkus originally appeared under the title "Flight" in *West Coast Line* (2012). A modified version of "Bird" appeared in *TUFT* (BookThug, 2013).

"Elvis and Jacques" by Billeh Nickerson is from *Artificial Cherry* (Arsenal Pulp Press, 2014).

"Save the receipts" by Cecily Nicholson is from *Triage* (Talonbooks, 2011).

"Kerrisdale" by Miranda Pearson is from *Harbour* (Oolichan Books, 2009).

"First Night" by Meredith Quartermain is from *Vancouver Walking* (NeWest Press, 2005).

Excerpt of "Prayer" by Jamie Reid is from *I. Another. The Space Between: Selected Poems* (Talonbooks, 2004).

"un/authorized interjection" by Renée Sarojini Saklikar is from *children of air india: un/authorized exhibits and interjections* (Nightwood Editions, 2013)

Excerpt from "marble bubble bobble" by Jordan Scott is from *Silt* (New Star Books, 2005).

"Wild and Unwieldy" by Sandy Shreve is from *Cedar Cottage Suite* (Leaf Press, 2010).

"The Vacuum Cleaner" by George Stanley is from *After Desire* (New Star Books, 2013).

"The Wailing Machines" by Rob Taylor is from *The Other Side of Ourselves* (Cormorant Books, 2011).

"Entropic Ends" by Jacqueline Turner is from *The Ends of the Earth* (ECW Press, 2013).

"Between You and Me There is an I" by Fred Wah is from *is a door* (Talonbooks, 2009).

"Oscar of Between, Part 17A" by Betsy Warland is from *Oscar's Salon* (2014) on www.betsywarland.com.

"Tracey Calls" by Calvin Wharton is from *The Song Collides* (Anvil Press, 2011).

"fresh ancient ground" by Rita Wong is from *undercurrent* (Nightwood Editions, 2015).

"Tomorrow" by Daniel Zomparelli is from *Davie Street Translations* (Talonbooks, 2012).

STEPHEN COLLIS is the author of

Contributors

JORDAN ABEL is the Nisga'a author of *The Place of Scraps* (Talonbooks, 2013) which won the Dorothy Livesay Poetry Prize, and *Un/inhabited* (Talonbooks, 2015).

JOANNE ARNOTT is a Métis/mixed-blood writer, editor, and blogger, with nine published books in English. Born in Manitoba, at home in unceded Coast Salish territories for more than 30 years.

ELIZABETH BACHINSKY is the author of five collections of poetry, which have been nominated for literary prizes, adapted for stage and screen, and translated into numerous languages. She is the former editor of *Event* magazine and permanent faculty in the Creative Writing program at Douglas College.

DENNIS E. BOLEN, MFA, has published five novels and two collections of short fiction. He taught at the University of British Columbia, was an editor at *subTerrain* magazine for ten years, and a long-time editorial and arts writer for *The Vancouver Sun*.

GEORGE BOWERING is a veteran poet and fiction writer who lives in Vancouver. His latest book of poetry is *The World, I Guess* (New Star, 2015).

TIM BOWLING is the author of 12 books of poetry, four novels and two works of non-fiction. He has received numerous accolades for his work and has taught both poetry and fiction at the Banff Centre for the Arts.

COLIN BROWNE's most recent collection is *The Hatch* (Talonbooks, 2015).

STEPHEN COLLIS is the author of five books of poetry, including the Dorothy Livesay Poetry Prize–winning *On the Material* (Talonbooks, 2010). Collis is an activist and social critic, and also teaches contemporary poetry and poetics at Simon Fraser University.

WAYDE COMPTON writes poetry, fiction, and non-fiction. His latest book is *The Outer Harbour: Stories* (Arsenal Pulp, 2014). He is the director of the Writer's Studio at SFU Continuing Studies.

PETER CULLEY was the author of *Hammertown*, a long poem in three books. He published criticism since 1986, and recently had a show of his photography at the Charles H. Scott Gallery in Vancouver. He passed away in 2015.

JEN CURRIN has published four books of poetry, including *The Inquisition Yours*, which was a finalist for three contests and won the 2011 Audre Lorde Award for Lesbian Poetry. Her most recent book is *School* (Coach House, 2014).

PHINDER DULAI is the author of *dream / arteries* (Talonbooks, 2014) as well as two previous books of poetry. Dulai is a co-founder of the Surrey-based interdisciplinary contemporary arts group The South of Fraser Inter-Arts Collective (SOFIA/c).

DANIELA ELZA is the author of *the weight of dew* (Mother Tongue, 2012), *the book of It* (iCrow, 2011), and *milk tooth bane bone* (Leaf Press, 2013). She has lived on three continents and now calls Vancouver home.

MERCEDES ENG is a teacher and writer in Vancouver, unceded Coast Salish land. She is the author of *Mercenary English* (CUE Books, 2013).

MAXINE GADD is the author of *Subway Under Byzantium* (New Star, 2008), *Back up to Babylon* (New Star, 2006), and *Lost Language* (Coach House, 1982), as well as many chapbooks. She holds a BA from UBC, and lived on the Gulf Islands before settling into her adopted community in Vancouver's Downtown Eastside.

HEIDI GRECO works in nearly every genre, from essays and reviews to poetry and fiction. A long-time resident of Surrey, she served as the city's "resident poet" in 2012. Her work has been published in numerous anthologies, and her most recent full-length book is the novella, *Shrinking Violets* (Quattro Books, 2011). She works as an editor and instructor.

HEATHER HALEY is a poet, author, musician and media artist. She is the author of two poetry collections and her work has been featured in numerous journals and anthologies. Her debut novel is *The Town Slut's Daughter* (Howe Sound Publishing, 2014).

RAY HSU is author of two award-winning books of poetry, *Anthropy* (Nightwood, 2004) and *Cold Sleep Permanent Afternoon* (Nightwood, 2010). He has published more than 150 poems in more than 50 publications worldwide. He is a creative writing instructor.

AISLINN HUNTER is an award-winning poet currently working on her third book of poetry. She also writes fiction. Her latest book is a novel called *The World Before Us* (Doubleday, 2014). She lives in North Vancouver.

MARINER JANES is the author of *The Monument Cycles* (Talonbooks, 2013), and *blueprint*, a chapbook. While studying at SFU, he co-edited *iamb* magazine, a venue for new and emerging writers. Mariner works in Vancouver's Downtown Eastside.

REG JOHANSON is the editor of CUE Books and a writer and teacher on unceded Coast Salish Territory, Vancouver, BC.

WANDA JOHN-KEHEWIN is a mixed-blood Cree writer originally from Kehewin, Alberta. She is a graduate of SFU's The Writer's Studio, and her first book of poetry is *In The Dog House* (Talonbooks, 2012).

RAHAT KURD's first book of poems is *Cosmophilia*, published by Talonbooks in 2015. She lives in Vancouver.

SONNET L'ABBÉ is from Waterloo, Ontario.

FIONA TINWEI LAM has authored two poetry books, *Intimate Distances* (Nightwood, 2002) and *Enter the Chrysanthemum* (Caitlin Press, 2009). She co-edited the non-fiction anthology, *Double Lives: Writing and Motherhood* (MQUP, 2008), and edited *The Bright Well: Contemporary Canadian Poetry about Facing Cancer* (Leaf Press, 2011).

EVELYN LAU is the award-winning author of 11 books, including poetry, non-fiction, short stories, and a novel. Her most recent collection, *A Grain of Rice* (Oolichan, 2012), was shortlisted for the Pat Lowther Award and the Dorothy Livesay Poetry Prize.

CHRISTINE LECLERC writes poetry and prose. She is the author of *Counterfeit* (CUE Books, 2008) and *Oilywood* (Nomados, 2013) and served on editorial collectives to produce *portfolio milieu* (milieu press, 2004) and *The Enpipe Line* (Creekstone Press, 2010). In 2014, Leclerc received a bpNichol Chapbook Award for *Oilywood*.

DONATO MANCINI is the author of several books of poetry, most recently *Loitersack* (New Star, 2014) and *snowline* (eth press, 2015). Mancini's collaborative visual works have been exhibited worldwide. He is currently enrolled in the PhD program at the University of BC.

DAPHNE MARLATT has been writing and publishing for four decades. *The Given* (McClelland & Stewart, 2008) won the Dorothy Livesay Poetry Prize. She was awarded the George Woodcock Lifetime Achievement Award in 2012.

SUSAN MCCASLIN's recent volumes of poetry are *The Disarmed Heart* (The St. Thomas Poetry Series, 2014) and *Demeter Goes Skydiving* (University of Alberta Press, 2012), which won the Alberta Book Publishing Award. McCaslin's chapbook, *effortful / effortless: after Cézanne*, is forthcoming from Alfred Gustav Press in 2015.

KIM MINKUS is a poet with three books of poetry: *9 Freight* (LINEbooks, 2007), *Thresh* (Snare Books, 2009), and *Tuft* (BookThug, 2013). Most recently, her work appeared in the anthology *Best American Experimental Writing 2014* (Omnidawn Publishing).

CECILY NICHOLSON is the author of *Triage* (Talonbooks, 2011) and *From the Poplars* (Talonbooks, 2014), which won the 2015 Dorothy Livesay Poetry Prize.

BILLEH NICKERSON is the Vancouver-based author of five books. His newest poetry collection is *Artificial Cherry* (Arsenal Pulp, 2014). He is the Chair of the Creative Writing department at Kwantlen Polytechnic University.

JULIANE OKOT BITEK is a Liu Scholar and PhD Candidate at the Interdisciplinary Studies Graduate Program at UBC. She thinks a lot about home, exile and diaspora. Her research interest is on social memory and national identity.

CATHERINE OWEN lives in New Westminster and is the author of nine collections of poetry, among them *Frenzy* (Anvil Press, 2009), which won the Alberta Book Prize. Her most recent publications are a book of elegies, *Designated Mourner* (ECW Press, 2014), and a chapbook, *Rivulets: Fraser River Poems* (Alfred Gustav Press, 2014).

MIRANDA PEARSON was poetry mentor at SFU's Writer's Studio from 2004-2007. She is the author of four books of poetry, most recently *The Fire Extinguisher* (Oolichan, 2015).

MEREDITH QUARTERMAIN often writes about places and their history. Her most recent books are *Rupert's Land: a novel* (NeWest Press, 2013), and *I, Bartleby: short stories* (Talonbooks, 2015).

JAMIE REID was a writer, activist, and one of the co-founders of *TISH*, an influential poetry journal. His recent work includes *I. Another. The Space Between* (Talonbooks, 2004) and *homages* (pooka press, 2009). He published *DaDaBaBy*, a magazine of local and international avant garde writing. He passed away in 2015.

RACHEL ROSE is the current Poet Laureate of Vancouver, and a former SFU Writer's Studio Poetry mentor.

RENÉE SAROJINI SAKLIKAR writes *thecanadaproject*, a lifelong poem chronicle that includes poetry, fiction, and essays. The first completed book, *children of air india: unauthorized exhibits and interjections* (Nightwood, 2013), won the 2014 Canadian Authors Association Award for poetry.

JORDAN SCOTT is the author of three books of poetry, including *Decomp* (Coach House, 2014), a collaboration with Stephen Collis and the ecosphere of British Columbia. He lives in Vancouver.

SANDY SHREVE's books include *Waiting for the Albatross* (Oolichan, 2015), *Suddenly, So Much* (Exile, 2005) and *In Fine Form: The Canadian Book of Form Poetry* (Caitlin Press, 2005), co-edited with Kate Braid.

GEORGE STANLEY has published seven books, most recently *Vancouver: A Poem* (New Star, 2008). He is the recipient of the 2006 Shelley Memorial Award for Poetry and a board member of *The Capilano Review*.

ROB TAYLOR is the author of *The Other Side of Ourselves* (Cormorant, 2011), poetry editor at *PRISM international*, and one of the coordinators of Vancouver's Dead Poets Reading Series.

JACQUELINE TURNER has published four books of poetry with ECW Press, most recently *The Ends of the Earth* (2013). She lectures at Emily Carr University of Art + Design.

FRED WAH has published 24 books of poetry, fiction, and non-fiction. The publication of *Diamond Grill* (NeWest Press, 1996) placed him as a prominent figure in writing race in Canada and abroad. He is the current Parliamentary Poet Laureate for Canada.

BETSY WARLAND's most recent book, *Breathing the Page: Reading the Act of Writing* was a bestseller. She is the author of eleven books of poetry and creative non-fiction. For excerpts from her work-in-progress, *Oscar of Between*, go to www.betsywarland.com.

CALVIN WHARTON is Chair of the Creative Writing department at Douglas College. He is a former editor of *Event* magazine, and writes poetry and fiction.

RITA WONG is the author of four books of poetry, the most recent of which is *undercurrent* (Nightwood, 2015). Her book *forage* (Nightwood, 2007) won the 2008 Dorothy Livesay Poetry Prize. Wong is an Associate Professor in Critical + Cultural Studies at Emily Carr University of Art + Design.

CHANGMING YUAN started to learn English in China at 19 and currently edits *Poetry Pacific* with Allen Yuan in Vancouver. Changming's poetry appears in more than 1000 literary publications worldwide.

DANIEL ZOMPARELLI is the Editor-in-Chief of *Poetry Is Dead* magazine. He is a co-podcaster at *Can't Lit*. His first book of poems *Davie Street Translations* was published by Talonbooks. His collaborative poetry book with Dina Del Bucchia, *Rom Com*, is forthcoming from Talonbooks, fall 2015.

Acknowledgements

We want to express our heartfelt appreciation to everyone involved in bringing this book to publication. Our thanks to Monica Miller, who managed the book from beginning to end. As well, many thanks also to Brian Kaufman, Karen Green, and Shazia Hafiz Ramji at Anvil Press.

We value the ongoing support of Shauna Sylvester, Robin Prest, Kim Gilker SFU Public Square, and the entire hard-working Lunch Poems team, past and present. A special thank you to Dr. Laurie Anderson, executive director of SFU Vancouver.

And finally, our sincere gratitude to the poets who create—and the readers who contribute to—a vibrant and engaged community.

In Memoriam

Peter Culley (1958–2015)

Jamie Reid (1941–2015)

SFU PUBLIC SQUARE

lunch poems AT SFU

FREE Lunchtime readings the third
Wednesday of every month featuring
well-known and up-and-coming poets.

Teck Gallery
Main Floor
SFU Harbour Centre
515 West Hasting Street
Vancouver, BC

www.sfu.ca/lunchpoems

SFU

SIMON FRASER UNIVERSITY
ENGAGING THE WORLD

THE WRITER'S STUDIO
SFU VANCOUVER'S
CREATIVE WRITING PROGRAM